The Future of the
Jewish People in
Five Photographs

Peter S. Temes

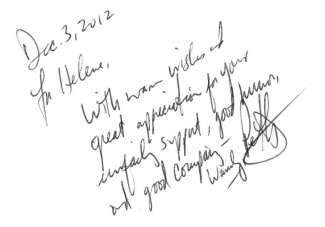

University of Nebraska Press
Lincoln and London

Photo credits: p. 36: Photo by Millard
Rogers, courtesy of the Cities and Buildings
Database, University of Washington, http://
content.lib.washington.edu/buildingsweb;
p. 45: Photo collected by Bishop Charles
White, circa 1910; p. 74: AP Photo;
p. 104: Bettman/Corbis (U1309142B);
p. 144: Anthony Weiss/ *The Forward*.

Library of Congress
Cataloging-in-Publication Data
Temes, Peter S., 1966–
The future of the Jewish people in five
photographs / Peter S. Temes.
p. cm.
Includes bibliographical references.
ISBN 978-0-8032-3979-1 (cloth: alk. paper)
1. Judaism. 2. Jews—Identity. 3. Jews—
United States—Identity. 4. Jews—Civiliza-
tion. 5. Temes, Peter S., 1966– I. Title.
BM565.T46 2012
305.892'4073—dc23
2012004215

Set in Sabon by Kim Essman.
Designed by Mikah Tacha.

This book is dedicated to Irving and Eleanor Rempell, and to Lloyd Temes. As always, Judy Temes has been my first and most exploited audience, and my partner in reflection.

Many teachers and wise men and women have helped me think through the ideas presented here. Rabbis Fred Greene, Irwin Kula, and James Prosnit deserve special thanks. My dear friends Ilan Stavans and Uri Cohen have been rabbis of another kind to me as well, and I thank them most sincerely.

Contents

Illustrations

Eyeh Asher Eyeh

As a boy in Brooklyn, I discovered early on that each of the subtribes and microcommunities in my Jewish world had its own approach, distinctive and richly flavored, to the past. One collection of stooped uncles (most of them actually *uncles* of my uncles) was always neatly dressed for business in dark wool jackets and ties, smelled of a range of tobaccos, and would stand around in modest family-gathering living rooms holding plastic cups of seltzer and talking about the war or the family's departure from Russia or some recent business misadventure. They would quickly get to the point of *what really happened*, emphasizing the "really." "What *really* happened?" one of them would say to close a question just as it was opening. "I'll *tell* you! It was *enough*! So it's *over*. And that's *it*."

From another branch—this one hailing from Poland instead of Russia, a bit more urban and educated—came an entirely different emphasis: "What really *happened*," these taller, trimmer storytellers would say, stretching the "happened" into three or four words' worth of open vowels, "if I can *remember*"—another looping pretzel of sound—"was kind of a *mess*."

The Jewish look back, reluctant but irresistable to these old men and women who had lived through the worst of the twentieth century, felt to me like a boundary the old Jews of my childhood could not quite get past. Of the many qualities of grief in their intonation—no matter how jocular or generous they might be, they could never hide that grief—one certainly came from knowing that their shared past kept them from the full embrace of the most fundamental Jewish task, the task of looking forward.

Most of us wonder about the future, of course, and not only for the pleasure of imagining ourselves years from now, reinvented perhaps or happily the same. We also have vital questions—Will we be safe? Will we be happy? Will we be good?

When we turn specifically to the future of the Jewish people, we do more than play the game of imagination, and we carry more than the weight of prudent anticipation. The future is a special concern of Jewish people. When Moses climbed Mount Sinai and stood before the burning bush, he asked, "What shall I tell the people is your name?" The Hebrew answer to that question—*Ehyeh Asher Ehyeh*—has been translated in many different ways. Memorably, the voice of God in the epic film *The Ten Commandments* says, "I am that I am." That translation from the Hebrew began with the first Greek version of the bible, from the third century BCE, a translation carried forward in many of the most widely read English-language bibles ever since. But the literal Hebrew in the original is different. The words are in the future, not the present, tense. God tells Moses his name this way: "I will be who I will be."

The center of Jewish religious experience is, in fact, the God who is unfolding, who is in the process of becoming. That is what we worship. And so as we sit in our rooms today and ask, "What will become of the Jews?" we are are not talking about something beside or beyond the core of Jewish teachings. A central lesson of the Torah is that God is present in every place, in every moment in all the world, above us and beside us. If we reflect on the name of God—"I will be who I will be"—we see that the future is the very essence of Jewish religious experience. For all the emphasis on the thousands of years of tradition and for all the teaching about Jewish history, it is the *becoming*—not the remembering— that the Jewish God identifies with most. When we seek the divine in our lives and in the lives of others as Jews, we seek a quite specific kind of divinity. We seek the future.

■

The five photographs that, taken together, serve as the organizing principle of this book hint at possiblities of that future, possibilities hopeful and inspiring but also challenging and troubling.

The first two photographs ask us to consider the difference between religious experience and the countable facts of demographics. Does it matter whether there are more or fewer Jews? Is it perhaps more important to consider *how* we are Jews, rather than how many? Perhaps a single deeply, properly, powerfully *Jewish* Jew would mean more than a hundred or a million Jews who could all check the "I'm Jewish" box but do little more. Or does that emphasis on individual spiritual experience lead us away from the communal essence of Judaism? (The one-great-Jew theory, my friend Rabbi Irwin Kula insightfully points out, is very close to the story Christianity tells about its own superseding of Judaism, a story in which the one perfect Jew is named Jesus.)

The third photo asks about virtue: Is it enough to fight the good fight, even if we fail? Or must we win? Put another way, to what degree ought the Jewish people, in our efforts to help heal the world, keep our own status and well-being in mind, rather than pursuing virtue fully, at any cost? Golda Meir offered one answer to this question when she reportedly said to

Anwar Sadat, "We can forgive you for killing our sons. We cannot forgive you for forcing us to kill yours." To heal the world—to do the work that Jews must do—first Jews must survive, she suggests, even with a loss of innocence and a loss of virtue that we find bitter and that diminish us spiritually. This balance between survival and virtue remains one of the most contentious questions about Judaism across the world. How we answer it as individuals affects our families and our communities. How we answer it as a people affects whether there will be very many Jews at all a few generations forward.

The fourth photo extends these questions about virtue to the role of Jews governing a Jewish state and asks about the exercise of practical power as a special challenge to all that is best about religion.

And the last photo asks about the difference between the meaning we *put in* to the sacred Torah scrolls through our worship and the meaning we *take from* those scrolls. As we gather to read, to hold, and to cherish the Torah, are we encountering a set of stories and commandments that are complete in their own terms, that we are to understand and obey, or are we entering into a dialogue with the Torah, interpreting and reinventing it as our communities grow and change?

It would be enough for many Jews if these scrolls were our source of power and faith because in them we can find our fathers and mothers, Moses and Sarah, the Jews of Egypt and the Jews of ancient Israel. And as we consider the scrolls as objects, as the pillars of worship through past centuries, they hint at the lost Jews of a hundred nations: the Jews cast out of Spain, the Jews of Poland, the Jews of the camps. Our familes, for generations, have poured so much into the scrolls through their worship. Even if the scrolls were empty, even if the scrolls were entirely outdated or simply wrong in their teachings, they would still hold enormous and irreplaceable meaning built by every pair of hands that has ever held a Torah.

But from another perspective, this meaning is merely a beginning, barely approaching the essense of the Torah, which taken on its own terms is nothing short of God's presence touching our lives and forming the subtance of the world.

Focusing on what we put in to the Torah offers a tolerant and expansive view of Jewish identity—if not quite man creating God, then at least men and women making choices about how God and Jewish identity suit them. It allows the richness of Jewish tradition, the comfort of Jewish affiliation, and an embrace of Jewish history, without demanding submission to God or in fact much else. The contrasting perspective brings with it the power and wonder of divinity, but it also closes many doors. The final photo forces us to consider which of these alternatives holds a better future for the Jewish people, or perhaps which will allow any long-term future at all. And it might suggest, hopefully, the prospect of the integration of these two alternatives, a making whole of otherwise separate extremes. "The reason God gave us two tablets," one rabbi recently told me, "was to give us the job of integrating them and making them into a single, usable whole."

■

The relatively happy circumstances of Jews in America over the past several generations have allowed many—perhaps most—American Jews to answer all of these questions without conceeding the fundamental choices and compromises that they will eventually demand. We have been able, more or less, to be in favor of strength *and* virtue. We have been able to say that we accept the Torah on its own terms, and also reshape it to fit the lives we lead. We have been strong voices in helping others, from the American civil rights movement to the moral catastrophe in Darfur, while not failing to help ourselves.

But the nature of the challenges to the Jewish people is clearly changing. The demographic engine of intermarriage and assimilation is no longer a prediction but a long-established fact. The moral compromises of occupation and coexistence in Israel are today starker and more closely watched by world powers, established and emerging, than they have been in at least a generation. The forces driving Jewish continuity in the home and in the world at large are in many ways weaker than they have ever been, while the private and public pressures *against* Jewish continuity seem to be gathering force.

One economist, a professor at an Ivy League university, presented the challenge to me this way: "Reason won't support the Jewish future. If you think like an economist, you see that the incentives for being Jewish, in practical terms, are much smaller than the incentives for becoming part of the dominant religion in the larger community most of us live in. It just makes more sense not to be Jewish in any kind of serious way, and the exit door is wide open, with nice-seeming people saying, Come on, we love you, step through this door. So it's not reason that will keep Jews Jewish. It has to be faith. We don't just have to *know* that we're Jewish; we have to *feel* it."

THE FUTURE OF THE JEWISH PEOPLE
IN FIVE PHOTOGRAPHS

CHAPTER ONE

How Does It Feel?

□   □   □   □   □

The feeling of being Jewish in the United States has never been simple, or fixed. It's astonishing, in fact, how different being Jewish has felt generation to generation in the places I've lived.

Two of my great-grandparents—my mother's grandmother, called Bubu, and her husband Jamesie—were typical of their generation, arriving in New York shortly after the turn of the century as teenage immigrants in the crowded, cobblestoned streets of New York's Lower East Side, a Jewish ghetto of tightly packed tenements. Men and women dressed in the black jackets and long, coarse skirts of eastern Europe filled the sidewalks. Half the goods to be bought in the area—fruit, pickles, fish, clothing, pots, and pans—were sold from wooden pushcarts; the rest, from storefronts with Hebrew lettering spelling out Yiddish words over every other shop, English woven through for the sake of clarity in some cases and confusion in others.

They had met as children in Poland and fell in love as young adults in New York. Married, they moved to the West Bronx, another Jewish ghetto though less dense, with cleaner streets and a cheap apartment with more rooms for a family that would include four children. Every neighbor was Jewish; every store in their neighborhood served a Jewish clientele; and Yiddish and English and Polish—to say nothing of Latvian and Russian and Romanian and Hungarian and Czech—gave the public spaces a linguistic tumult distinctly Jewish, distinctly eastern Eurpean, and distinctly American.

Bubu (her name a variant on the Yiddish word for grandmother) and Jamesie (his American name born of his habit for describing any object he could not say in English a "Jimjick") never went to *shul*. "Never. Not once," my mother recalls. But the shul they did not go to had a pariticular character. They were not avoiding an airy suburban temple, as I might today, or a communal hub sanctioned by a Polish governor and supported by a tax levied on all Jews in the disctrict, as their parents might have. They failed to attend a specific kind of shul—small, presided over by a rabbi who had likely traveled from Lodz or Minsk or Krakow with a knot of townsmen and their families, renting cheap space for cramped services in Hebrew shaped by the inflections of dialect Polish and local Yiddish. They didn't attend, but they would have heard the language of this worship, would have heard of the rabbis, would be known by their neighbors not to attend—just as the majority of their new American Jewish neighbors did not attend.

They were consciously nonworshipping Jews, but they were Jews absolutely. And being Jewish felt like being part of a nation within a nation. Jamesie was a waiter, always in New York's Lower East Side kosher restaurants. If he had to defend his habit of abstaining from worship, it would most likely be over the sabbath dinner table with relatives or at a Passover seder. If he didn't say the prayers, he certainly knew them.

And Bubu, who did not work outside the house, cooked

every day and for every holiday meal—every *Jewish* holiday meal. They both spoke English with heavy accents, and they went to Jewish doctors, Jewish grocers, Jewish bakers, Jewish weddings, Jewish celebrations of the birth of a new son (the bris always held on the eighth day of life and including the ritual circumcision to affirm the child's place in the Jewish covenant with God).

What did being Jewish feel like to them? It must have felt like a life raft, something to cling to in the sea of American culture, a way to trust the local merchant and a common bond with the man who might offer you a job. It must have sounded like the intonations of a family dialect and tasted like food at a ritual dinner hinting back at generations of continuity, all offering some degree of comfort even in a radically new place.

My grandmother—daughter of Bubu and Jamesie—and my grandfather were both born here, and both witnessed as children the social realities of the Great Depression. My grandfather, seventy years later, would weep as he recalled seeing neighbors go hungry. For this generation, the feeling of being Jewish involved more choices. Like their parents, my grandparents too avoided worship; and like their parents, they also lived in a thoroughly Jewish world. Still, they ventured outward in ways their parents did not.

In the 1920s and '30s, they were the first generation in their families to attend public schools, schools with mostly Irish and Italian and Yankee teachers, mostly women. Poor performers, then, were firmly asked to leave school—to go find work, which was legal in the 1920s and '30s for even the youngest children. As they grew older, my grandparents became aware of the edges of their Jewish identities in ways that their parents, firmly fixed in the Jewish immigrant world for work and play and politics, were not. My grandfather became a union organizer on the docks, cheek by jowel with Irish and Italian unionists (and antiunionists). My grandmother and her sister joined the Earl Robinson People's Chorus, an interracial singing society dedicated to progressive politics as seen through the lens of the American Communist Party. My grandmother, finishing high school, went to work as a clerk at a public hospital, working with every variety and persuasion of New Yorker imaginable.

My grandfather, having bitterly left school at sixteen to help support his parents and siblings, agonized over whether to join up with the Abraham Lincoln Batallion of the International Brigade, to sneak into Spain and fight against Francisco Franco's Fascists, along with two thousand other American Communists and Socialists, many of whom were Jewish and many of whom were not. To be Jewish, he felt, was to have a conscience, to fight for what you believed in, to strike a blow on every occasion possible for the man on the bottom of the pile.

He stayed in the Bronx, adding his paycheck to his family budget, while his best friend went to Spain and died. Forty years later, he and I played a game of paddleball—a game I've only ever seen played in New York—in the park near our homes in Brooklyn. My mother had moved out of her family's upstairs apartment on Exeter Street to settle with my father in a home on Coleridge Street (the blocks in my neighborhood ran alphabetically, named after the schools and poets and shires of England). My grandfather always wore a bulky ring, the metal forming a knot across the top, and he had put it in his pocket before we began our game of slapping a hard, black ball against a single, stark concrete wall with wooden paddles not too distantly removed from cutting boards. Then he stopped. He'd lost his ring. He searched for half an hour, not panicked but deeply troubled. The ring had been his friend's gift before going to Spain. He told me a little about his friend and the cause in Spain, but his mind was on the ring; his feeling of loss was almost overwheling.

The ring reminds me that for much of my grandfather's generation in New York, being Jewish meant being part of a small world nested in a larger one. Being Jewish in his time and place meant a Bronx Yiddish tone to his English and a street around the corner with a kosher butcher, a hat shop that sold yarmulkas, and an appetizer store specializing in herring and pickles; but it also meant meant a more engaged kind of politics, life in public schools, and unions. It meant certain songs, as well as language and foods and neighborhoods. None of these flavors and feelings of Jewish life for him were simple, and many remained painfully incomplete. He'd loved his American school but had to leave. And he was never sure he had made the right decision about Spain. The waterfront union to which he devoted a decade of his life—and some of his blood—was a triumph, but also a failure: wages went up, the workweek went down, and workingmen claimed a strong voice, but the union was soon notoriously corrupt, eventually the subject of the film *On the Waterfront*.

In the next generation, things were very different. For my parents, many of the hinted promises that the prior generation had heard were unequivocally fulfilled. Their generation of Jews, born in the decade before the Second World War, by and large stayed in the public schools—and in New York they were very good schools. Their teenage years arrived in the postwar boom. Very few felt the economic weight that bent so many of their parents; and after finishing high school, they found public colleges that were putting aside their restrictions against Jews, cost little or nothing, and rewarded the cultural habits of closely reading texts and arguing the meaning of details that Jewish learning had valorized for five hundred years.

5

My mother's father and my father's father had not attended a traditional Jewish *beit midrash*—house of learning—where the rabbis wandered as referees through small rooms packed with pairs of students facing each other across long tables arguing the textual fine points of Torah and Talmud; but *their* fathers had, and their fathers before them, part of a chain stretching back for generations. What each new generation learned over the dinner table, carrying that culture forward, was strikingly well tuned to the academic machine creating a new postwar American professional class. *Pay attention to the details. Read, and read more. Make your case. Challenge your peers, but respect authority. Argue carefully.* These Jewish habits, carried over from the yeshivas of eastern Europe and the remnants of Jewish Babylon and Spain, helped Jews of my parents' generation feel that large swaths of the world—at least the parts of the American world most of them lived in—would reward them for their work, not only in spite of their Jewishness, but in some ways because of it. While the horrors of the Holocaust cast their shadow over this generation—I can recall my father crying after he helped carry my Hungarian father-in-law's casket, later saying that he was so moved by the privilege to bury a survivor, "at least, one that Hitler didn't kill"—the very darkness of Europe would highlight for many the pure good fortune of being Jewish in America instead of being Jewish anywhere else. That they might have been something else in America certainly did not occur to my parents, though they too seldom went to shul.

My parents were both born in Jewish neighborhoods—real American ghettoes with Yiddish still in the air, close quarters, and stores that people from other neighborhoods seldom shopped in and would have found hard to understand:

Barrells of pickles? Tongue sandwiches? A store window full of *tallises*? But when my mother was a teenager, her parents moved from the Bronx to the far side of Brooklyn, near the ocean. Their younger daughter, my mother's only sibling, often had trouble breathing, and her doctor prescribed ocean air and less crowded streets. My grandparents moved to the upstairs apartment in a private house. The neighborhood had been built originally as a summer colony for Manhattan's wealthy. By the time my grandparents arrived with their two daughters, it too was a thoroughly Jewish neighborhood but with a broader range of Jews than they'd lived among before. It remained a ghetto only as a matter of religious demographics: it was a prosperous place, Jewish doctors and Jewish lawyers living beside schoolteachers and shopkeepers who had spent perhaps a little more on their homes than prudent; though, even there this generation had the wind at their backs, as the extraordinary rise in New York real estate beginning in the 1970s led many to think themselves small-time financial genuises. My father was one of the schoolteachers; his friend Marty across the street was another. Both earned PhDs at night, course by course, their incrimental bumps in pay with every new credit completed outpacing the cost of graduate school tuition and adding up over time. When my parents bought their small home in 1968, my mother didn't work. The family already included two children and would soon add a third. They paid $38,000. Forty years later, my mother sold that house for $1.2 million.

Being Jewish in my parents' generation was a complex feeling. They were still outsiders in some ways—and more so in some places than in others. But as their world changed, as education became the vital passport to the middle classes and as the middle classes prospered as they never had before, as the material benefits of being an American in the middle of the twentieth century became more and more clear, being Jewish took on a new dimension. In some ways, it felt *lucky*.

My father certainly felt this luck, in fact all too much. I can remember gratitude and wonder in his voice when he sat on the couch in the upstairs apartment my wife and I rented in the Brooklyn nieghborhood where my parents both still lived—each in their own house, though, after their divorce; my mother was in the family home from 1968, and my father in the house he bought in 1979 (he bought it for $125,000 and sold it in 2000, for $1 million, still lucky).

"Can you believe it?" he asked, as a room full of us took a break from admiring my new baby daughter, the first of the nine grandchildren my sisters and I would eventually raise in Brooklyn, the Bronx, Manhattan, New Jersey, Massachusetts, Illinois, and Florida. "A guy like me," my father continued, "can take $50,000 and turn it into $1 million." He was talking about a real estate deal, the largest in a series of smaller ventures that had taken the equity in his house and his share of my mother's and parlayed it all into ownership of a thirty-family aparment building, home mostly to welfare recipients, a few blocks south of a trendy neighborhoood whose borders were stretching in that direction seemingly month by month.

My father was going to sell the aparments as co-ops. He was already counting the money. This was 1988, and the real estate bubble that had multiplied his net worth unstoppably through the 1970s had already begun retreating from its peak, though few as yet understood that, certainly not my father. "No one," he had told me a few years earlier, as he was beginning to borrow on his homes to buy small investment properties, "has ever lost money on real estate in New York." Even as a teenager, I had a pretty good feeling that he was wrong. Years later, we could remember that remark around a holiday table and toast my father with a warm smile: "Here's to the first man who ever lost money on real estate in New York."

And he lost a lot of it—all he had, in fact, though by then he was not nearly as broken by his financial reversal as he might have been earlier. After my parents divorced, his net worth still rising, I helped my father move into an apartment over a shop in a small apartment building he had bought on the edge of our neighborhood. It had been a low-income building—a genuine dump—for generations, and he took pleasure making himself at home there. "I really don't need much," he told me. "Money is for the family. And look at you, you're all doing great." His emphasis on family was certainly a mark of his generation of American Jews, though my parents' 1970s divorce was one as well.

I asked my father once, when I was in high school, why he had become an engineer. "I wasn't smart enough to be a doctor," he told me. "And an engineer was the next best thing to make a good living." I was stunned to hear that. My thoughts about the future were all about finding a calling, doing meaningful work. Making a living—something I took for granted—was not part of my calculus. It was striking to think that it had been the entirety of his. Money was not suspect as a motive for my father because he had learned that money, at its essence, is family. It was what a good father used to build a wall to protect his wife and children, to give them choices, and to make them all strong.

All this he understood as Jewish, but Jewish in a special way—certainly not religious. Once, he told me, "You have to understand why I love Puerto Rican people so much," and this was at a moment in the history of our city when Puerto Ricans were often maligned and the Puerto Rican gang movie

The Warriors—really a decline-and-fall-of-New-York propaganda film—had just come out, its action taking place two neighborhoods away in Coney Island. My father said, "I love them because when I was a kid, Jews were Puerto Ricans." Look at the jobs these people have, he would tell me, look at how hard they have to work, listen to the accents, notice how other people treat them. In his childhood, Jews played a similar role. Even my father's English had a slight hint of Yiddish to it, and the older men and women in the neighborhood of his childhood had heavy accents. Jews were normal citizens in their own buildings, their own streets, their own shops; but they were keenly aware of being outsiders elsewhere. Some jobs were off-limits. True, if there were private clubs, restaurants, and hotels that were similarly restricted, they hardly felt it, because when did they go to clubs, restaurants, or hotels? My father's point was that to look at Jews from an outsider's perspective in the 1940s must have felt a lot like looking at Puerto Ricans in the 1970s. Perhaps the elders didn't think much about their role in the larger public life of the city and country because they were so fully engaged in their families' survival, but their children certainly would. For my father, being Jewish felt in the end like being a winner, but he understood that the game kept on and others deserved the same chance to fight and win as well.

Yet, for my father, feeling Jewish had almost nothing to do with feeling the presence of God. Going to shul was an experience in nostalgia for him. He took me on two occasions to an ultraorthodox shul when I was a boy, and I did have a bar mitzvah. But we rarely went to temple otherwise.

My mother's experience was different. Like her parents, she'd been inside synagogues only for family functions, and she seldom thought of Judaism as connected to God. Like her parents—and my father—she felt thoroughly Jewish. Yet when she divorced at forty, she told her friends that she hoped her next husband would be like Mr. Rogers, the children's television host. I don't think she recognized that Fred Rogers, a Christian minister, was about the most distinctly un-Jewish man one could find. Her second husband, in fact, turned out to be a tall, trim, soft-spoken Christian from Iowa. He was a kind and dedicated husband and precisely the man you'd want central casting to send over if your principal need was "not a Jew." Yet my mother felt something in Judaism that her parents and my father never really did. She felt a spiritual tug. She wanted to encounter God.

My parents had both taken the civil rights movement very seriously; and while they were a little old to be part of the 1960s counterculture, they were drawn in small ways to its spirit. Beyond the notable Jewish presence in the movement—beginning with the extant news clips of students dancing the hora during the occupation of a building at the University of California at Berkeley at the launch of the free speech movement in 1963—a strand of underground Judaism was there on the margins and caught my mother's attention. Similar to the Jesus movement that became a small part of the counterculture, the quieter Jewish parallel took the form of a growing consciousness of outside-the-shul worship, and included a strong feminist perspective. A number of *havurahs*—organized worship groups with an iconoclastic feel, often meeting in members' homes—were launched by young rabbis and students, including one led by Art Green neear Boston. Green had published an essay in 1968, "Psychedelics and Kaballah," that connected his visions while taking LSD with Jewish spirituality. Green made the connection between radical youth culture and Jewish religious experience in no uncertain terms. *The Jewish Catalog*, a book I recall finding in my living room as a boy, had a similar place at the juncture of Jewish sprituality and the explosions of alternative culture, consicously paralleling the Ken Kesey–inspired *Whole Earth Catalog*, something of a hands-on how-to guide to alternative living in America.

As a divorced woman, a professional with a career and a home with children growing up feeling that every door in the world might open for them if only they knocked, my mother wanted things her parents had not thought to want. She was not rich but could make the money she and her family needed to live comfortably. She was not politically naive, but she was no radical and took no communal comfort in protest or political struggle. It was being Jewish that held a promise of spiritual community, something she came to value more and more as she moved through her life. She became more reflective, thought more about God, and was an engaged visitor to any number of shuls and temples. She loved the hard-core Orthodox for their passion and the completeness of their faith, but she had no interest in following their rules. She enjoyed Reform and alternative services for their openness and their tolerance. She never joined a new synagogue, and she kept her sense of Jewish sprituality as a private commitment, something to share with friends who felt it too but something apart from much of the rest of her life. She could call on Judaism when she needed it, when she felt pulled to express gratitude or to find refuge and strength; but it made very few demands on her. It was a kind of bonus, laid on top of a largely happy and prosperous life.

■

I think often about that economist's comment—that the future of Judaism hinges on how it feels to be Jewish. For me, the feeling of being Jewish has been different at different times—and places—in my life. The Brooklyn I grew up in was a very Jewish place. Through grade school, being Jewish was the norm. But junior high school, in a building across a footbridge that seperated our neighborhood from the rest of Brooklyn, was a place that required a degree of caution. The economic and cultural cleavege that made my friends and I targets of the older, tougher students from other neighborhoods—eighth and ninth graders held back long enough for some to have full beards and blue-collar part-time jobs—fell along religious lines, but it took a while for us to notice. Even college in upstate New York meant a colony largely of young New Yorkers and our cultural cousins from other cities and suburbs. Only as I began to travel for business jobs after college and later as a teacher and lecturer in small towns did I feel far enough from home to understand my Jewishness as a mark of real difference. When I'd visit a college in rural Ohio for example and hear from my host that the FCA really dominates the culture of the campus, later learning that FCA stood for the Fellowship of Christian Athletes, I'd wonder how they might interpret my New York vowels and gestures, even my small beard. But one could never know the answers. I keep in mind Jackie Mason's line: I'm not a racist; I don't like you *personally*.

■

In Connecticut on the edge of the New York City commuting bubble, I drove one night some years ago with my two teenage daughters. We were coming home after a visit to my parents and my sisters, all living now in New Jersey. We talked about how the growing branches of my family are different today, and about how we're similar. We talked about being Jewish, something that my daughters feel in a very different way than I did at their age.

Counting about 20 percent of the population as Jews of

some variety or other, our town is far more Jewish than most of the others in our strip of Connecticut suburbs. That's still a small enough proportion for my daughters to feel that to be Jewish is to be a little bit different. Both of my daughters went to temple, went to Jewish camps, were bat mitzvahed—but each act of belonging has been an active choice that has meant a step away from a circle of school friends or a sports event on a Jewish holiday. Our daughters are now far more learned in Jewish prayer and history than I am because of their studies at Hebrew school and summer camps. They've stepped decisively toward Jewish identity in ways that I—and most of the people I grew up with—seldom had to.

On that car trip, we also talked about what it means to be a rabbi. My younger daughter had been thinking about it as a possible career path. At that momemt, I'd been thinking about it too. My life as a teacher of literatue and ethics had led me to learn a great deal about Christian philosophy and to encounter a fair number of Christian clerics whom I'd admired. My daughters had heard me say before that, were I a Christian, I'd already be a minister, though as a Jew I thought I would not become a rabbi, because the role of the rabbi is in some ways fundamentally different, with more duty to preserve, defend, and carry forward the faith. That did not sound like me.

But that night on a quiet country parkway, both my daughters challenged me—we think you don't really know enough to say that, they told me. And I decided they were right. That kicked off several months of serious study of Hebrew and Jewish scripture, and about a year later I applied to the rabbinical program at a Jewish seminary. By the time I heard of my acceptance, though, I was already sadly back to where I had started: this was not for me. My sense of Judaism as a spiritual path was exactly that, a path toward the divine. Because I am a Jew, my path toward God will be a Jewish path, but the universal human experience of divinity is clearly the glowing aspiration. Yet at every step, I found the idea of Jewish peoplehood woven into the spiritual duties of the rabbi and rabbinical student, even to the point of every Jewish seminary in the United States wanting to know the religious history of my wife and her family. Many would not enroll a candidate who had married outside of Judaism. And all the seminaries wanted to know each applicant's feelings about Israel, some quietly making it clear—and some not so quietly—that a commitment to the state of Israel was a requirement. My motive, my sense of calling, was about Judaism as a religion, but there was something more built into the rabbi's role in the seminaries I applied to: the rabbi as a particular kind of communal leader, still playing something of the role of the civic authority that the priest had been in biblical times and that rabbis still played in much of Europe through the early twentieth century as the larger political establishments would cede local governance of the Jews to the rabbis and Jewish councils in exchange for a collective tax and enforcement of often onerous laws of separation and servility.

At that point in my exploration of rabbinical study, being a Jew felt to me like bearing a complicated history on my back. I looked—without success—for a collection of fellow Jews who wished to put down the load while still trying to follow a Jewish path toward God and who also happened to have a rabbinical school.

Later, while driving that same road in Connecticut, I found myself heading home alone one evening after a light snow. My lights lit up the road directly ahead of me but not much farther. Then for a moment I heard the sound of rain, and it stopped. Then came a sharp, green smell: pine tar, eucalyptus. The snow in front of me became, for a moment, a carpet of green. I saw a thin chimney of steam rising along a tree on the other side of the road, over the barrier. In another moment, it was all behind me. It took me a minute or two of dazed driving, moving quickly away from that dark scene, to understand what had happened. A car had hit a tree. The tree took the hard blow, and the force of it moved up and out along its branches, pine needles shooting out by the thousand, each trailing a drop of green pitch and filling the air with that smell, then blanketing the snow.

I'd passed close by someone else's tragedy, while tasting the sticky pine smell of fresh life. The questions I asked automatically—Am I in danger? What's going on? Can I help?—are certainly not especially Jewish questions, but a moment like this does test us and reveal us. I kept on driving. I didn't panic, but I didn't first think to try to rescue anyone (and was hardly equipped to the task, if I'd wanted to). I came away with a feeling that I should do more. More importantly, I should *be able* to do more. The unexpected illumination of the dangers in the familiar, and the realization that someone might have died that night while I felt able to do nothing more useful than dial 911, told me that I'm too comfortable with my own comfort, so secure and removed from the suffering of others that I should work harder to see the troubled places where I might do some good. I suspect that this feeling might in fact be the most distinctive addition by my own generation to what it feels like to be Jewish.

CHAPTER TWO

How Much Change Can Judaism Stand?

□   □   □   □   □

Religious worship has always had two sides to it—comfort and affliction. Congregation and community, setting down our worldly and spiritual burdens, feeling the presence of God—this is the comfort of worship. But in most religions, the creator is demanding as well as forgiving, will punish as well as bless. Jewish prayer says again and again that God is great, God is mighty, and God is to be feared. This is Soren Keirkegaard's *Fear and Trembling* in the presence of God—something bone shaking. Religion would be half-empty without it.

In a culture that celebrates individual choice, consumer appetites, and freedom of religion, it is no surprise that many would choose to take the comfort and discard the affliction. Why not a Judaism of love alone, of forgiveness, of creation without destruction? And every possible permutation of a new Judaism is in fact preached and practiced, each having in common with the others at least one fundamental belief: we can change the rules to make Judaism fit our lives. It's up to us.

Hard-core believers respond forthrightly to this argument: God's demands and God's gifts are not ours to modify or mold. It would take more than a human lifetime to fully understand them; how foolish to believe that we can know them well enough to reject them.

Psalm 119 is the theological conservative's highest expression:

Thou hast ordained Thy precepts, that we should observe them diligently.

Oh that my ways were directed to observe Thy statutes!

Then should I not be ashamed, when I have regard unto all Thy commandments.

...

With my whole heart have I sought Thee; O let me not err from Thy commandments.

Thy word have I laid up in my heart, that I might not sin against Thee.

Blessed art Thou, O LORD; teach me Thy statutes.

From this perspective, we cannot reject any of God's statutes, because we don't yet truly know them. The Psalms present the moment of religious desire, of needing God. If religious feeling begins there, it has no room for judgment of God, because God's absence is still so keenly felt. Judgment and reason have nothing to do with this religious yearning. This is the feeling of an unsatisfied faith, a deep hunger for something we know exists and feel just beyond our reach, one descisive step away. "Make me to understand the way of Thy precepts: so shall I talk of Thy wondrous works,"

Psalm 119 goes on to say. We don't turn to God because we already understand God's path, and agree with it. We turn to God *in order to* understand. The yearning, the desperation of Psalm 119, is a desperation to take that step and be with God, through God's law.

But others hear this and say, What kind of spiritual journey is this—"teach me Thy statutes"? How about "teach me thy love, thy joy, thy greatness?" The statutes are the petty things. If we get the spirit right—the love and joy and transcendant greatness of God—why live in the small strokes of the law, praying precisely this prayer, while wearing exactly that garment, facing just this way, and eating only from this bowl for meat and that bowl for milk? We can do better. We can take the spirit of our religion, the wisdom at its core, and make it more usable for the lives we live today. We have a choice.

And in fact this choice is the major fault line that runs through the collectivity of the Jewish people today. Should we obey the Torah, or should we add our hands and minds and souls to it, shape it as it has no doubt been shaped in every generation past, to keep it relevent enough that our children will not turn their backs on it?

I think of one man I know, born Jewish, the son of Jews, who is perhaps the kindest and most generous person I've ever met. He earns money mostly so he'll have enough to give to anyone who asks for help. He spends time helping people he knows—his family, his neighbors—and a multitude of strangers he meets through community groups, walking down the street, or in the pages of his local newspaper. As soon as he feels that someone is suffering an injustice, he reaches out. And still he works a regular job and lives like an ordinary man; he could not stand to be seen as someone who feels exempt from the ordinary rhythms and compromises of daily life. He considers himself Jewish. "Of course I'm Jewish," he says. "Just look at me. Listen to me. From head to toe, I'm a Jew." But he also thinks of himself as a Christian. "I believe all of the Torah. I still study the Talmud. But I've turned the page. There's more to the Jewish tradition than you can expect if you turn your back on what comes after the Torah and the Talmud. Jesus is a great rabbi, and his teachings are our teachings. It's not different from Judaism; it's more, it's a step forward and upward.

"Look," he continues, "Judaism has the right answers, but it looks a little different today, because there's more to the whole thing than there was a thousand years ago. It's no different from the change that happened from the time of the First Temple in Jerusalem to the time of the rabbis in the Talmud. We learn more, we live lives that ask for new things from the scriptures, and we make something new but still built on the past. Judaism wins. We just call it something else today, something more. Everyone should be happy about that."

But, of course, not quite everyone is happy about that. "Turning the page" is a kind of revision of Judaism that is utterly false to many traditional Jews. They don't want anyone to create new versions of Judaism. Judiasm simply isn't Judaism if you don't do it in the most traditional way, according to the most conservative keepers of the faith. And if you are born a Jew, being Jewish in unsanctioned ways can be an immense moral failure.

"The fundamentalist view," writes scholar Samuel Heilman in the *Journal of Ecumenical Studies*, about the hardcore Othodox Jews, who stand at the extreme pole in this arument, "is that there is a single truth, that the people who share this truth are tied in an unbroken chain to the past, and that this truth is not limited to the private domain but can and should be imposed on the public square." He continues, "This truth is articulated as fundamentals of the faith, which must be practiced or believed if one is truly to be among God's defenders. . . . The fundamentalist assertion [is] that these essentials are tied to tradition, and often demanded by an inerrant text. . . . Fundamentalism is therefore often engaged in an intense battle against forces in the contemporary world that, in its view, seek to undermine or to defile the world as it sees it."

Contrast this to the Philadelphia synagogue that centers its outreach and member recruitment around the words of a congregant: "I feel that here I have permission to be the Jew I wish to be"; and the two sides of this argument are as clear as possible. Judaism is seen by some as a received religion with rules to be followed every day, derived from the Torah and enumerated in the Talmud. Judaism is seen by others as an evolving religion that allows us to change what needs changing so that we can be the Jews we wish to be, which for some will mean blurring the borders that mark the line between Judaism and atheism, Buddhism, Christianity, or any of a thousand other ways to live and worship.

A False Choice?

These are stark alternatives, and they are quite real. But perhaps focusing on the extremes leads us to imagine a false choice. A view that allows some change but not all change, that distills the spirit of the old laws while striving to find the line between enough change and too much, has enormous appeal. This kind of compromise—not a rejection of purity, but an embrace of two kinds of virtue, the virtue of tradition and continuity and the virtue of tolerance—speaks to many

Jews who feel caught between opposing camps. And after all, as Arthur Green writes, "exaltation and awe, joy and terror dwell together in prayer." It is the blending of extremes—neither softened—that makes some of the magic of religious experience.

Of course, if we discard the either/or of the "no change" or "all the change we want" readings of Torah, we may soon enough be avoiding extremes across the board. Instead of a choice between Jewish strength and Jewish virtue—the second of the two large conflicts in the self-understanding of the Jewish people—perhaps there is a unity to be uncovered on this issue as well. Perhaps finding some way of pulling the extremes together, as the rabbi conjuring an image of the two tablets integrated into one whole suggested, will be the great challenge of the Judaism of our age.

The future for the Jewish people, beyond the logical fizzle of demographic dilution, and beyond the perceived need to circle our wagons against the threats of cultural, familial, and political encroachment thus putting the needs of Jews above the needs of others, may well lie in rejecting the pro-or-con logic of strength or virtue, of holding fast to a literal Torah versus shaving its edges and trimming its shape to fit the modern styles of the modern Jew.

And the evolution of the main Jewish denominations in the United States in the past twenty years or so suggests that a middle path is indeed emerging, one that steers the communal experience of Judaism more fully toward the spiritually ambitious work of hard-core religion while also affirming the social and ethical substance of Jewishness. Where recent generations of American Jews crafted a virtue-centered Judaism by pulling back from the purely spiritual and religious, the current generation tilts the other way, back toward God-

infused worship while still declaring the ethical consicous-
ness of the books of the Prophets and the Talmudic idea of
healing the world to be the central organizing principles of
Judaism. Many find the rejuvinated religious intensity of the
Reform and Conservative movements to be signs of vitality
in Judaism. On the whole, God is more present in their worship than in recent decades, Hebrew is more present, and
traditional ritual is more present.

Yet outside the synagogues, the feeling and flavor of Judaism are less present in the typical Jewish home; and the typical Jewish neighborhood is not, itself, so typical anymore, because so few of these neighborhoods remain. And where the
pitched battle in American non-Orthodox Judaism, between
the advocates of Judaism as culture and the spiritualists who
would not relinquish their vision of Judaism as the extended
encounter with God for which we have been created, seems
in some ways to have eased, a closer look suggests the natural and sad peacemaking of a fading remnant rather than
real agreement—much as the town that once held a dozen
squabbling synagogues ranging across the spectrum of Jewish denominations now clings to one last remaining house of
worship, a Reformadoxative amalgamation in which arguments are unresolved but put aside in favor of more basic
questions of communal survival.

Less Focused, Less Polemical—Just Less

Jews may be less focused today on the Jewish civilization
as a replacement for the Jewish religious experience simply
because Jews are less focused, period. "Judaism as a civilization" is less of a thing to fight over because it appears to
many young Jews as a lost civilization of grandparents who

swam in their Jewishness in ways impossible today, an object of nostalgia and study. It has become less polemical because it is less vital, and just plain *less*, overall.

One place that vitality has gone is the sphere of ethical life that is not distinctly Jewish but recognizably Judeo-Christian—the secular public sphere in the West, settled on the principles of equality and virtue. These are important elements of Judaism in some of its forms, especially the Judaism of the Prophets, which emerges centuries after the Judiasm of the core of the Torah, the five books of Moses. Ask a Jewish American if all men are created equal—if all should be equal before the law, if all are equal in the eyes of God—and I suspect that most would be quick to say "of course." This is the foundation of the civic world we inhabit, the foundation of the laws we live under, and the foundation of the official and civic principles of tolerance that have made the United States and parts of postwar Europe such happy and decent places for Jewish people. We take these principles largely for granted; but if we wish them to be the pillars of our Jewish religion—or even if we wish them merely to be compatible with our Jewish religion—then that religion needs some reworking.

It will need to place an emphasis on virtue closer to its center and make fewer claims for the Jewish people as a morally and spiritually special group. Judaism, in sum, would need to become less about how the Jewish *people* can survive and thrive, and more about how Jewish *virtue* can expand and endure. This would be no small task, and one that might bode poorly for the future of Judaism as a religion. The Jewish people as individuals would likely do well enough, but they would, just as likely, be less and less Jewish, and rather quickly.

The Universal Ethic

If Judaism becomes a virtue-centered religion, it will likely not survive many generations longer, because Judaism is a minority religion with a good slice of the world's population specifically interested in seeing it end. Kindness to outsiders does not serve the interests of a besieged population. Judaism was born as a tribal religion, with a greater moral status for Jews than for others, an understanding well adapted to circumstance. The religion that one finds in the five books of Moses (and most especially in the fifth, Deuteronomy) served the interest of Jews more than it served the interest of humanity generally. Many Jews today don't like that fact and find great appeal in the universalism of modern ethical philosophy—particularly American Jews who take seriously the idea that all men are created equal. But this universalist ethic predicts the future of Judaism as a vestigial remnant layered deep inside other religions that will fully supplant Judaism, through a combination of love and hate.

Two current leaders of the Reform and Conservative movements, Jack Wertheimer (provost until 2007 of the Conservative movement's Jewish Theological Seminary) and Steven M. Cohen (research professor of Jewish social policy at the Reform movement's Hebrew Union College), pointed out in a 2006 article that "the classical formulation" of the special status of Jews "is in the biblical book of Exodus, where the children of Israel are commanded to serve at one and the same time as 'a kingdom of priests and a holy nation.'" To hold this view, though, is to compromise the modern ethical worldview that most of us cherish.

"I know that one has to pay a price for freedom," Hannah Arendt once told an interviewer, "but I cannot say that

I like to pay it." Arendt was speaking about the unpleasant strength that Western democracies needed to cultivate to survive during the Cold War. She could as easily have been talking about the future of the Jews as well. To survive, Judaism must pay a price—and Jews who want both the Enlightenment vision of spiritual equality and the continuity of Judaism as a vital religion that remains essentially Jewish will have to decide which side of this equation they are more willing to compromise or sacrifice.

The majority of Jews in the United States, Europe, and Israel already do not worship as Jews, do not belong to synagogues, and live much more visibly as citizens of their nations than they do as members of any religious community. Because we believe in the virtues of living as equals in democratic societies and because we are, therefore, troubled by a religious philosophy that pulls toward a special spiritual status for us and specifically not for others, we quietly step away from the Jewishness that holds its traditional shapes and contains its traditional ideas. The new kinds of Jewishness that we invent to fill the new holes, thus created, look more and more like the softer versions of the dominant religions in the nations that have tolerated and even embraced us.

Wertheimer and Cohen are acutely aware of this falling away. "Mounting evidence now attests," they wrote, "to a weakened identification among American Jews with their fellow Jews abroad, as well as a waning sense of communal responsibility at home. The once-forceful claims of Jewish 'peoplehood' have lost their power to compel." Jews have largely not swapped this sense of Jewish peoplehood for another brand of minority affiliation, but have in many cases accepted instead the philosophical universalism that became a central part of Western philosophy in the eighteenth century. The notion that God cherishes all of us equally whether we are Jewish or Christian or Buddhist or Muslim is not only different from the philosophies we find in the Torah, it is a threat to these philosophies. Judaism can change to accommodate these new ideas—and those of us who wish to be both Jewish and true to the humanist ideals of the Enlightenment want Judaism to accommodate them. But in the process, Judaism begins to look a good bit more like the Christianity that prevails throughout most of the West.

These are the two ideals that are impossible for us to reconcile: We wish Judaism to be universal in its moral outlook, as Christianity is, featuring a God who demands the same virtue from all without a special concern or special duty for one people but not another. But we also wish it to be, at its heart, the Judaism of our fathers and mothers, unchanged and unaltered in its power to connect us back through the generations. We can't have both; and if we try to make Judaism a *fair* religion—fair in what it demands from and provides to everyone—we will blur the lines between it and the other religions that already wish to embrace Judaism for their own purposes.

How Much Reinvention Can Judaism Take and Still Be Jewish?

Certainly, reinvention is a powerful part of religious experience. Even the most religious Orthodox communities do not follow the very letter of the Torah, though they might claim otherwise. Where they can, they often do—matters of cutlery and diet, as examples, hold strong to the ancient word. But who among even the most religious Jews will drag their disobedient children to the public square and stone them? Who will enforce a death penalty for planting the wrong crops in the wrong fields, or for gathering wood on the Sabbath?

Those on the fringe who might act out these ugly biblical teachings are seen by the vast majority of even the most traditional and committed Jews as mad.

The exchange and dialogue of the Talmud, the record of rabbinical debate and teachings dating in its two major constituent pieces from roughly the year 200 CE and 500 CE respectively, teach reinterpretation and reinvention through their very form and structure.

After the fall of the second Jewish temple in Jerusalem in the year 70 CE, rabbinic teachings that had been passed on through study, dialogue, and debate around the religious and political center of the Jewish nation were at great risk once that center was lost; and those teachings—based on the oral law, or oral Torah, that the rabbis long claimed to have been whispered by God to Moses, as a parallel to the written Torah he put into Moses's hands—needed, finally, to be written down. By the year 200 CE, Rabbi Judah ha Levi produced—the most common word used by scholars is "redacted"—a record of the rabbinic teachings, based on and parallel to the five books of Moses. This was called the Mishna. And around the year 500 CE, the rabbinic commentary on that work, called the Gemara, was added to it, to form the core of what today we call the Talmud (which refers particularly to the Babylonian Talmud, including the Gemara of the Babylonian rabbinical academies, as distinct from the earlier and less comprehensive Jerusalem Talmud). The structure of the Talmud—texts commenting on the comments on earlier texts—is at times raucous and almost always invigorating. Dialogue and debate thread around each page, and the presence of vibrant, committed voices parsing original texts and asserting their own interpretations is inescapable. From the chorus of voices in debate and, occasionally, in agreement comes the flavor of Jewish learning—the flavor of struggle, of making old teachings new, and of the communal act of creating meaning.

But here is one of the powerful contradictions that mark the path forward for Jews as a people. Rethinking, reinventing, and reinvigorating Judaism is vital for its future, and this impulse is an obvious fact through all of Jewish history. But the external pressures on Judaism and Jews pull the curve of reinvention toward the non-Jewish norms of other religions that are hungry to exert exactly that influence, because of their own universal visions.

This is dangerous work. The imperative to examine and reinvent is essential to Judaism, yet many of the ways in which we might change pose existential threats to Jews and Jewishness. Change is the mandate; but do it this way instead of another, the cost of getting it wrong might be absolute. Another reason, as some of the older Jews of my childhood might remind us, it isn't easy to be a Jew. But who says it should be easy?

The Quickest Path to a Future without Jews

The 11 million or so Jews in the world today do not, of course, collectively decide on how to be Jewish or on strategies for Jewish survival. Certainly there is no shortage of committees and assemblies that try to do this kind of thing—and then, of course, councils of heads of the committees, committees of the heads of the councils and so on—but the very proliferation of so many groups declaring themselves Jewish leaders and claiming Jewish authority testifies eloquently to the lack of a single, central voice for the Jews of the world and the lack of a single institutional hand to guide the motion of the Jews as we move toward our collective future. Yet we are always moving toward the future; and through the millions of small choices that we make, we chart an observable course. Most of the ways in which we can understand that course reveal a story of almost inevitable decline. The story of the Jews looks a lot like the story of any one of hundreds of once powerful and growing religions that are today more or less gone.

Marking Boundaries

There is an undeniable vibrancy to the Orthodox movements that hold most firmly to their view of the Torah as divine and fixed in its meaning. Yet their own narrow views force them to rule out the large majority of Jewish people from the category of true Jews. Put aside the obvious millions who do not meet the strictest matrilineal tests of Jewishness, even though they feel and live as unequivocal Jews (my wife and three children fall in this category). Any number of Orthodox groups, including the influential Orthodox Union, are in the habit of announcing that Reform and Conservative congregations are not truly Jewish. At the other extreme is the mainstream Christian view that Judaism is still alive and well—indeed, perfected—through the deliverance of the Messiah. If we do not allow fundamental reinterpreting of the Torah, we become a narrower (and much smaller) band of hyperbelievers; yet if we loosen our sense of the Torah's boundaries and borders, we may become unrecognizable as Jews, regardless of our protestations. But the compass points on this issue are clear: change always conquers stasis, given enough time. Reinterpretation has been going on since the first moment that Judaism existed. The question at issue is where to draw that boundary—to say *this* we can change, but *that*, never, because that is the essential piece of Torah that makes Jews Jewish.

Our lives are easier—and in many cases, our communities and places of worship are fuller—if we allow the widest latitude for reinterpretation of Torah so that any Jew can feel not only Jewish culturally but religiously as well, because the religious substance of Judaism is flexible, welcoming, and tolerant. But without fixed borders of interpretation, even as more and more people claim to be true to the Torah they move the Torah itself—or their interpretation of it—across the line that separates Jewish from non-Jewish, as in the case of the many millions of Christians who understand their own faith to be the perfection of biblical Judaism.

If we mark that boundary too closely to biblical Judaism, it won't fit the post-Enlightenment world that we live in and, generally, wish to defend against fundamentalists from other religions who are often remarkably hostile to Jews and Judaism. If we mark that boundary too far from biblical Judaism, we take a big step toward Judaism's eventual fading into something different, a dialect of other languages rather than a language of its own. This is clearly the greatest challenge in thinking about a future for the Jewish people.

■

I wish I could say that my reflections on tradition and faith have led me to hold the views that might offer the Jewish people a good bet for a long future, but I can't. Like many Jews, I grew up with some exposure to synagogue and traditional Jewish teachings, and I've never doubted my Jewish identity. But I have always felt a strong resonance with the fundamental ideas of the American experiment. Early on I came to feel that in the Declaration of Independence "all men are created equal" means equal before God and before the law—and I've held tight to this notion of equality all my adult life. As a matter of personal faith, this suits me well and deeply. And while the truth of this idea is arguable for the political philosopher, it is not arguable for the traditional Jew. Jewish men are different; they have different obligations under the laws of the Torah and a different relation to Jewish law (which means to be an all-encompassing law) than non-Jews do.

My American identity clashes terribly with the traditional Jewish identity some would have me hold more dear, but I am not sure why I feel that mis-fitting so distinctly. Is it because I spent more time in the public schools of New York City than I did in the synagogues of my neighborhood? Or because at some level, I hear Kant, Jefferson, and Martin Luther King, and I feel an absolute rightness in their moral view? Is my wished-for comfort as both a Jew and an American undone by nurture or by nature? I can't tell.

Perhaps the contradiction is not as great as I sometimes feel. I can certainly find lines from the Torah that predict the later emergence of a universalist moral outlook, but these attempts seem not very different from finding in the Torah predictions of the coming of Jesus. There maybe be something there, but it seems mostly a matter of our wanting it to be.

My problem is that my personal convictions place me behind the Jewish caravan, pushing hard as it tips over the cliff. I feel the Enlightenment faith in humanity and equality as an absolute faith. All men and women *are* created equal before God and the law, in my view. And while I do accept that strength is, at times, more important than virtue, this is not a conviction I feel good about; and I find myself rejecting it—almost always—in my practical judgments of politics and policy. While I cherish the traditions and the teachings of the Torah, I don't cherish all of them; and I do see the hands of men in those scrolls at least to the same degree as I see the hand of God. I know the Torah has been reinvented from its earliest origins and will be again, sometimes too much perhaps. But I don't doubt that the reinvention will continue.

■

I am a classic enemy of my own people's future: successful enough in my integration with the larger world that I dislike the question of whether anything is good for the Jews, because I subscribe to the idea that good for you means good for me, if I live my life ethically enough. Except, I know, too, that this modern outlook, this university-bred equalitarianism, sits right beside the too-quick and overly clever observation that Judaism is essentially over, the only real question being whether the endgame takes five generations or twenty.

Of course, another side of me recoils at this, recoils with the same emotional illogic that melts my heart when I hear some of the old cantorial melodies that stuck to me from the few visits my father dragged me on to the ultra-Orthodox basement shul on the edge of our Brooklyn neighborhood. The past that I mourn is not really my past; but it is close enough that I can feel what is no longer there and (I hate to admit it) regret the sweet and shallow tunes that I have heard among the Scandinavian woodwork of suburban temples as a beardless rabbi reaches for his guitar. Something lost, something gained—but more is lost than gained, I think, along the steep slope we are continuing down.

Should we try to halt the slide? Should we put aside the new knowledge that every soul is equal, that the good things are universally good, that the Jew is no better or worse than his neighbor of a different faith simply because he is a Jew—with no greater call to do God's work, no greater call to live in God's land, no greater privilege or burden—because we have finally figured out that what we once cherished as the extraordinary unearned blessing and curse of living as a Jew turns out, in our new understanding of the world, to be the unearned blessing and curse of living as a man, or as a woman, and that's it, no more?

■

There is in my mind the gray-bearded, black-hatted image of the wisest rabbi, the rabbi who combines the most rigorous passion for Jewish tradition and worship with an unbridled love for all people. This imaginary rabbi combines, for me, the wisdom of Jerusalem with the wisdom of Brooklyn—the wisdom of the one genuine gray-bearded, black-hatted rabbi I encountered as a child with the wisdom of my insightful, secular grandmother, the wisdom of the heart with the wisdom of the mind. This rabbi has an answer. "So what should you do?" he asks, reflecting and affirming my question. "You want to be everything to everybody—you want to be in the world, but also in the *shtetl*. You want too much, but this is the way you are. You can't help it."

I can hear him saying, simply, "Be good. Be good because when you are good, you are a good Jew. And one good Jew is no small thing."

From the Behistun Inscription: "Says Darius the king:
Within these countries what man was watchful, him who
should be well esteemed I esteemed; who was an enemy,
him who should be well punished I punished; by the grace
of Ahuramazda these countries respected my laws; as it was
commanded by me to them, so it was done. Says Darius
the king: Ahuramazda gave me this kingdom; Ahuramazda
bore me aid until I obtained this kingdom; by the grace of
Ahuramazda I hold this kingdom."
–*Translated by Herbert Cushing Tolman*

CHAPTER THREE

The First and Second Photographs

■   ■   □   □   □

I met a man in New York a few years ago and decided to learn everything I could about him. We had a business meeting scheduled; knowledge would be an advantage.

I knew he had a senior job with a big media company, and I knew he was from India. To my surprise, Google pointed me toward the newsletter of a local Zoroastrian society. Zoroastrian families from New Jersey smiled in the photographs; a summer camp for Zoroastrian children announced its new season. This man—his name was Homi—was a leader in the community.

I wouldn't have guessed that there were enough Zoroastrians in the United States—or, frankly, in the world—to support a summer camp. Or even a newsletter. Yet when Persia was arguably the greatest empire in the world, it was a Zoroastrian empire. Under the emperor Darius, in the sixth and fifth centuries BCE, the Persian Empire stretched from the edge of India in the east to the Caucasus Mountains in the north and the Balkans in the west. Scholars of the period estimate that at least 3 of the 10 million inhabitants were believers in the religion founded by Zarathustra, worshipping a unitary god, Ahuramazda, focusing on good works and active expression of virtue in daily life. (Darius's predecessor, Cyrus, freed the Jews from their captivity in Babylon, and supported the building of the Second Temple in Jerusalem.)

This first photograph is of a stone carving on a mountainside in Iran, on Mount Behistun, near the town of Jeyhounabad. Carved in 520 BCE, roughly 45 feet by 75 feet and 300 feet up a sheer rock face, it depicts Darius, bow in hand, foot planted on a defeated rival, as subjects of his empire look on, their hands tied and necks roped together. It is a frightening expression of political and military power, made especially vivid because of the personal scale of the carving— not armies in the distance, but a handful of men, victims and victor, master and slaves. The figure farthest on the right, also enslaved, was added as the carving was finalized, representing a newly conquered nation brought under the reign of Darius during the year of the carving's construction. Once the carving was complete, the ledge below it where artisans had stood and steadied their ladders was hammered off the face of the cliff so that later rulers would be unable to reach and revise—or destroy—the carving.

Below, above, and beside the carved figures, columns of text tell the story of Darius's conquests over the subjugated people and their kings, in three languages: Elamite, Babylonian, and Old Persian. The names of the kings matched, as well, the text from early Greek historian Herodotus's widely read history of the period—and so early scholars had a local version of the Rosetta stone, a way to decipher a set of ancient languages largely gone from collective memory.

The rise of Islam more than a thousand years after the rule of Darius had a devastating effect on the Zoroastrians of Persia. After an Arab invasion in the seventh century CE,

Zoroastrianism was effectively banned. Many Persian believers migrated to India, and many others converted. Today, the global population of Zoroastrians is about 200,000, most in India, some in Iran, and about 20,000 in North America. It's worth noting, too, that when there were 3 million Zoroastrians, the world's population stood at roughly 100 million. At about 3 percent of the global population, Zoroastrians represented the equivalent of 90 million people in today's world of 6 billion.

■

The photograph frames the stone carvings between a broadening base, almost architectural in its seeming sturdiness like a pedestal hung in the air, and the rough stone in the upper right of the photo, hanging over the tableau, creeping over its border and emanating cracks in the stone that look almost like lightning bolts. The inscriptions add a sense of order—they stand in columns mostly across the bottom of the photograph but appear also in odd bits and pieces across the plane of the carving, neat columns and squares popping up here and there, narrating the image they inhabit.

Looking at the photograph of the Behistun Inscription, it's difficult not to think of the Tower of Babel, a story that comes and goes very quickly in the Hebrew Bible, in the space of a few lines in chapter 11 of Genesis:

And the whole earth was of one language and of one speech.

And it came to pass, as they journeyed east, that they found a plain in the land of Shinar; and they dwelt there.

And they said one to another: "Come, let us make brick, and burn them thoroughly." And they had brick for stone, and slime had they for mortar.

And they said: "Come, let us build us a city, and a tower, with its top in heaven, and let us make us a name; lest we be scattered abroad upon the face of the whole earth."

And the LORD came down to see the city and the tower, which the children of men builded.

And the LORD said: "Behold, they are one people, and they have all one language; and this is what they begin to do; and now nothing will be withholden from them, which they purpose to do.

Come, let us go down, and there confound their language, that they may not understand one another's speech."

So the LORD scattered them abroad from thence upon the face of all the earth; and they left off to build the city.

Therefore was the name of it called Babel; because the LORD did there confound the language of all the earth; and from thence did the LORD scatter them abroad upon the face of all the earth.

The Tower of Babel becomes a kind of treasure box in Genesis. Its builders abandon it, locked out by the confusions of multiplying languages. Off they go, scattered across the face of the world. But if the complexity of human language becomes a lock laid across the tower, the Behistun Inscription presents itself as a key. It tells us that while the top layers of language may push away outsiders, underneath there is a common humanity to the word. Languages fit together, if you know how. They tell the same stories; and if you know the stories in one language, you can learn the workings of others. You can open the lock.

And as with language, so with religion: there is a human center that connects the experience of different peoples, different tongues, and different kinds of worship of different kinds of gods. The move from one language to many does not have to be a curse; and the move from one supreme conception of God to many, the expanding outward of religious experience, can be something more than the losing of a single true path. This idea is central to the conflicting visions of Judaism as it exists today, and as it may continue on into the future. It is hotly contested, and the images of the Tower of Babel and the Behistun Inscription are helpful guideposts in making sense of the questions ahead of the Jewish people.

■

Among students of religion, Zoroastrianism is the archetype of the lost religion—ancient, once powerful, now largely forgotten. And I'm hardly the only Jew who thinks about Zoroastrianism when I think about the future of my own religion.

From one perspective, the future of Judaism is not hard to see, and not terribly hopeful. Demographically, Jews around the world are relatively well educated, relatively prosperous, and relatively egalitarian in terms of educational and professional options for women. People who study population trends agree that each of these three characteristics tends to lower the birthrate. Because of these virtues, Jews have fewer children than they otherwise might. And like Zoroastrianism, Judaism is not a proselytizing religion. If a prospective convert comes to a rabbi and asks to convert, tradition demands that the rabbi turn the prospect away three times before beginning an often difficult conversion process for those who persist.

Put simply, old Jews aren't creating new generations of young Jews at a quick enough pace. Deaths generally outpace births. And in the United States—home to 5 million Jews, about 40 percent of the world population—roughly half of all young Jews marry non-Jews. In those couples, more than half raise their children as non-Jews. In Israel, home to another 40 percent of the world's Jews, the non-Jewish citizens are generally poorer, less well educated, and less egalitarian in gender roles than their Jewish neighbors. Predictably, they have children at a much faster pace.

The trends seem straightforward: generation by generation, there will be fewer and fewer Jewish people in the world, and eventually Judaism will go the way of Zoroastrianism. ("Ah," people will say, "the Jews! A remarkable ancient faith. I'd love to meet one of the last Jews.") This is not merely a prediction about the future; it is a description of the present. Even without physical destruction, the current generation of Jews is nurturing a smaller follow-on generation, leading toward a likely end to the Jewish people if the trend does not turn around. The very root of the word "generation" draws us back to the Torah, to Genesis, as we undo the work of the creation of the Jewish people.

Like many Jews of my generation, I've seen this issue play out in my extended family, beginning with the urgings of a particular aunt of my father's whom we'd see at family weddings, urgings that seemed odd and wildly out of context. "We want you to stay in our club!" she'd say, with a too-wide smile. I might have been ten years old the first time I heard this, my sisters twelve and five; and we were baffled by this adult behavior in extremis. Within a few years, though, there would be weddings she did not attend—the weddings with a rabbi *and* a minister. And then more weddings without her, as the lines hardened. She might boycott one wedding, and then in retaliation she would not be invited to the wedding of the brother or sister or the close cousin.

I have eight cousins. Six are married. Two married Jewish women. Two married non-Jewish women. Two married non-Jewish men. And the two who are not married don't think of themselves as particularly Jewish. Their father—my uncle—is Jewish, but their mother is not. That wedding was one of the first my father's aunt did not attend.

When I married, I had not thought much about my wife's religion. She was—is—Jewish, and our three children have grown up with a strong sense of Jewish identity, certainly stronger than mine when I was a child. I grew up in New York City when the mayor was Jewish, when our local congressman was Jewish, when most of my teachers and just about all of my neighbors were Jewish. Feeling Jewish, at least demographically Jewish, was easy. My children have lived in several places, most with unusually large Jewish populations— our current suburban town is about 20 percent Jewish—but none of these residences have ever approached the Jewishness of my New York, the New York of the 1970s with deteriorating schools, growing crime, and dirty streets, but also with a sense of Jewish normalcy now largely gone even there and impossible to find elsewhere on such a large scale outside Israel. (When my family went to Israel for my bar mitzvah in 1979, one of the running jokes was to say, "Isn't it amazing! A place with 4 million Jews! Where else on earth could this happen! Well, maybe Brooklyn . . .") My children are always aware of their minority status as Jews in a way that I never was until I became an adult. This makes their Jewish identity stronger, but it also makes clear to all of us that we are standing, as Jews, on a shared but steadily shrinking platform. We aren't suffering, but we're a little nervous.

Reflecting on my family's position as Jews in America today, I certainly don't think of the dark times of the twentieth century—or come to think of it, of the nineteenth century, or the eighteenth century, and endlessly back. I do think, though, of what I learned about the Jews of Kaifeng, China, when I traveled there five years ago.

■

The second photograph shows two Chinese Jews reading a Torah protected by a round Torah holder in Kaifeng. The photograph was taken in 1910, when a small number of Jewish families remained in Kaifeng, an interior city that had once been the imperial capital. Several writers have made the claim that one thousand years ago, Kaifeng was the most important city in the world; and like so many important cities, it was home to a vibrant Jewish community, originally drawn from North Africa and Spain along the overland trade routes that passed through the area.

By the time this photograph was taken, the Jews of Kaifeng looked entirely Chinese, according to a feature in *National Geographic* in 1907. Clearly, intermarriage and cultural assimilation had had their impact. And by the time I found myself in Kaifeng, visiting with leaders of Henan University to hear about their plans for the future, I was surprised to be seated at a dinner party next to the university's professor of Jewish studies (I'd had no idea that there had been a Jewish community in that city and not a clue that Jewish studies was a discipline at the university). I learned that this gentleman was himself not Jewish; knew no Jewish people other than those who, like me, had passed through on other business; and had very little connection with the Jewish world.

No blood, no camps, and no armies had been necessary for the vanishing of the Kaifeng Jewish community. The Jews of Kaifeng had lived in peace, built businesses and families, gathered and prayed, married and had children—and then, one day, there were no Jews left. Two stone carvings from the seventeenth century, when there were several thousand Jews still in Kaifeng, mention the Jewish community there. Today they sit in the Henan historical museum like tombstones. This, in microcosm, is the fearful vision of the demography of the Jewish people.

The Second Photograph

And yet no religion is, at its root, about demographics. Rather it is the quality and not the quantity of Jewishness that is the fundamentally religious question about the future of the Jews. The counting of Jews, one could say, is a distraction from the religious essence of Judaism. Writer Leon Wieseltier captured this perfectly when he wrote recently about the parallel question of Jewish political allegiance: "Judaism is not liberal and it is not conservative; it is Jewish."

If Judaism is first and last a religion, not a political party concerned with how many votes or how strong a network of influence it might claim, then the central question of the future of the Jews is a question about humanity's relation to divinity and the ways that we can live our lives with meaningful connection to the eternal, not the future of how many Jewish houses of prayer we can find, or how many Jewish doctors or Jewish neighborhoods. From the religious rather than the demographic perspective, Judaism is a path and not a destination.

This perspective was eloquently summed up by Rabbi Marshall Meyer, leader of New York's B'Nai Jeshurun synagogue in the 1990s. Amid debate over a distressing National Jewish Population Survey in 1990, Meyer wrote, "there has been deep concern with Jewish continuity and with the survival of the Jewish people. Let us begin by asking, survival *as what?*"

The twentieth century brought this conflict of perspectives

45

—between those who emphasize the number of Jews and those who emphasize the spiritual substance of Jewish experience—into high relief. After the Holocaust, the political, practical, and demographic questions of Judaism were starkly clear. The rebirth of Israel as a political state posed intense questions about the connection between Judaism as a religion and Jewishness as something more, or something different. No shortage of Jews opposed the state of Israel on religious grounds, some because they felt that biblical prophecies were clear that the new Israel should be the work of the messiah and not the work of ordinary men and women, and others because they believed in the separation of church and state (some for the sake of the state, others for the sake of the church). Political questions about the Jewish state draw enormous (and deserved) attention, but they reflect and extend a more fundamental conflict about the Jewish religion, the conflict between Judaism's devotion to divinity and Judaism's devotion to Jews.

The arguments among Jewish movements (the term of art for the major denominations of American Judaism in the last hundred years) have paralleled this conflict and are most visible in the philosophies of the two newest.

■

The emergence of the Reconstructionist movement beginning in the 1930s, with its emphasis on Judaism as a civilization, framed a set of questions about what Judaism might be *beyond* religious experience, and those questions echo in secular Jewish-identity and ethical-culture communities. From the socialist Yiddishkeit Workmen's Circles to the Humanistic Judaism movement, a strong and enduring commitment to Jewishness, *with or without* prayer as a Jew, *with or without* a rabbi or a shul, has made itself clear, particularly among the majority of the world's Jews, who are in fact unaffiliated with any synagogue.

Mordechai Kaplan was the founder of Reconstructionist Judaism, which has risen in recent years from its status as a fringe alternative to the "big three" Jewish movements (Reform, Conservative, and Orthodox) and is today widely viewed as the fourth, claiming its own well-regarded seminary and hundreds of affiliated congregations in the United States and elsewhere.

Kaplan was born in Lithuania and graduated from the Conservative movement's Jewish Theological Seminary in 1902. He led a liberal Orthodox congregation in New York City, and in 1909 he became a full-time faculty member at the Jewish Theological Seminary. He paid particularly close attention to the work of John Dewey, who was then on the faculty at Columbia University. In 1920 Dewey published a book called *Reconstruction in Philosophy*, which called for a continual rethinking of orthodoxies of all kinds. Speaking about moral questions, Dewey wrote that traditional religion "hindered the operation of scrupulous and unremitting inquiry."

With this kind of inquiry in mind, Reconstructionism has become the branch of Judaism that takes the least for granted. In one sense the most liberal of the Jewish movements—because of its emphasis on reinventing the essence of Judaism from the bottom up, all the time—it has also become, in some ways, the most demanding, not only emphasizing study of Hebrew and Aramaic texts but also inviting a level of thought and personal choice easier to duck in more structured kinds of Jewish practice.

With its emphasis on asking questions over giving answers, what then does Reconstructionist Judaism believe? Kaplan's answer is clear in the title of his most influential book, *Judaism as a Civilization: Towards a Reconstruction of American-Jewish Life*, published in 1935 (Kaplan's debt to Dewey is certainly clear; the very word "reconstruction" is borrowed).

Kaplan recalls German poet Heinrich Heine—born Jewish but converted to Protestantism—writing that Judaism is not a religion but an affliction. Kaplan emphasizes the traditional languages, literature, and culture of the Jewish people. Most importantly, he writes deeply about Jewish ethics. Kaplan accepts a serious challenge in Heine's joking cosmology. Judaism is not only a religion, but more. That "more," if neglected, becomes an affliction. But if embraced, it can become a civilization that lifts the souls of those within it.

The Reconstructionist document "Who Is a Reconstructionist Jew?" offered today on the movement's main website as an official presentation of Reconstructionist philosophy, includes this important passage:

The Past Has a Vote, Not a Veto.

We struggle to hear the voices of our ancestors and listen to their claim on us. What did this custom or that idea mean to them? How did they see the presence of God in it? How can we retain or regain its importance in our own lives? We [also] believe "the past does not have a veto." Therefore we struggle to hear our own voices as distinct from theirs. What might this custom or that idea mean to us today? . . . When a particular Jewish value or custom is found wanting, it is our obligation as Jews to find a means to reconstruct it—to find new meanings in old forms or to develop more meaningful, innovative practices.

Reconstruction's embrace of the old is vital to its character as a movement meant to preserve as well as to reinvent. But the starting point of the movement has long been a quest to understand the experience of *the Jewish people*—rather than a quest to understand or, better yet, to experience God. This is where theology meets demography. In its approach to the Jewish People (capital letters in front of both words), Reconstructionism seeks to understand the *Jewish* through the lens of the *People*. With such a strong emphasis on Jewish civilization, this relatively young, growing religious movement must note with particular sadness the diminishing numbers of Jewish people, even as its own proportion of the Jewish population expands.

Importantly, Reconstruction has greatly changed in the past twenty years, and fewer and fewer Reconstructionist leaders today embrace the original Judaism-as-a-civilization position that Kaplan so explicitly laid out. Reconstructionist rabbi Les Bronstein, in fact, recently published an article that began this way:

If you advertise yourself as a Reconstructionist rabbi, people will inevitably corner you with "the" question: "Can you tell me—*in a few words*—what Reconstructionist Judaism is all about?"

In formulating a response that I could quickly pull out of my back pocket, I long ago decided not to lead people into the abyss of "two civilizations," "vote-not-a-veto," and other cul-de-sacs of Reconstructionist jargon. Instead, I like to approach the question by mentioning three arms which are vitally central to every form of Judaism, and I try to show people how Reconstructionist Jews (and, truth be told, a myriad of Jews around the world) view these matters in a way that is different from traditional Judaism, but surprisingly close to the spirit of that tradition.

The radical language of Kaplan's Deweyan movement has become for Bronstein—and many others—"an abyss." And the "three arms" he extends turn out to be the Talmudic trio of Torah, prayer, and mitzvot, the collective essence of Judaism presented in the cornerstone section of the Talmud, the Wisdom of the Fathers, dating from about 200 CE. So what's different, as Bronstein suggests? To begin with, "Reconstructionist Jews see the Torah as the Jewish people's response to God's presence in the world (and not God's gift to us)." So God is not the creator of the Torah but is its prompt or cause. God is the central presence to which Jews respond. The Torah created in response is divine in its inspiration and its aspirations, but not in its creation. And the fact that the Torah is now so vital to the Reconstructionist Jewish experience that Bronstein explains would be a surprise to Kaplan.

Prayer is equally important—and an equal departure from Kaplan's concerns—but "We believe that we are the primary respondents to our own prayers," Bronstein writes, "and that we need prayer to remind us of the Godly values behind our benevolent actions in the world." Finally, Bronstein writes that "God does not choose the Jews to be performers of the commandments. Rather, the Jews choose to be called by God."

God has returned to the center of this distinctive form of Jewish consciousness, but on man's terms. Human experience and human facts remain central, though the notion of what it is to be human has changed—the new Reconstructionist individual is God-infused, if not necessarily God-created.

■

The Jewish Renewal movement, younger than Reconstruction, supports a network of a few dozen congregations, most meeting in members' homes or borrowed halls. It faces the demographic crisis of Judaism from a different perspective. In its own core documents, Jewish Renewal does specifically acknowledge (in a tip of the hat to Reconstructionism) the importance of Judaism as a civilization, but it goes on to emphasize the experience of divinity and personal spiritual transformation in ways that Reconstructionism does not.

At its core, the Renewal movement is "rooted in Judaism's prophetic and mystical traditions," finding its center in the experience of God and the personal transformation of worship. The movement's official mission statement says that "The Jewish Renewal movement is dedicated to the Jewish people's sacred purpose of partnership with the Divine in the inseparable tasks of healing the world and healing our hearts." The theology of Jewish Renewal suggests, then, that personal religious experience and broader social justice issues are more important than the demographic crisis of Judaism.

Of course, one can easily say, "I worry about the disappearance of the Jewish people and Jewish civilization," while also saying, "The central task for Judaism is to connect with God." But there are choices to be made. The first is whether an individual ought to try to take action in face of the declining population of Jews. Many Jewish parents emphasize the importance they feel for their children to marry Jews. Yet the conflict between Jewish demography and Jewish spiritual experience may stand in particularly high relief here. What are we teaching, really, when we teach our children that Jews are better—there is no other way to phrase it—as marriage partners than others? Does this reflect the set of values we wish to hold as Jews today?

That question is as old as the story of Abraham, not only the first Jew, but also the first Jew to take pains that his son would marry within the faith. But that phrase itself, "marry within the faith," makes the contradiction clear, because it is not faith—that individual passion and dedication—that makes one demographically Jewish. Most often it is the unchosen fact of who one's parents were.

Would we want, for example, to say that marrying an un-observant, unreflective, perhaps unethical Jew is in any way better than marrying a non-Jew filled with the desire to heal the world, who lives generously and passionately? If we say, "Well, it's not so stark a choice, all of one or all of the other," then where exactly do we draw the line? How much do we weigh the technical fact of Jewishness over the actual living of a good and generous life? A little? A lot? Maybe half?

The ethical absurdity is clear. We must decide: are we more concerned with the fate of the Jews as Jews, or are we more concerned with a universal sense of what is right and what is divine? We must say either that Jewish identity is the essence of Judaism or that a set of values and orientations to-ward God are the essence, whether called "Jewish" or called another name.

■

I can remember sitting at dinner with a cousin, a young man doing very well in his first job at an investment bank in New York, a city far from his home in Atlanta and his college in Florida. We were talking about his colleagues and the quick decisions he has to make about whom to trust when making all kinds of formal and informal deals. "And, yeah, it goes without saying that I'll trust someone who's Jewish a little bit more than someone who isn't." I was surprised—partly because I'd had more than a decade of experience across a few different businesses and his preference didn't compute for me: my lived experience suggested that any factor be-yond the explicit evidence of trustworthiness was a distrac-tion. But my surprise also had something to do with the fact that this was a well-educated, fully assimilated, largely unre-ligious young man. He was a son of privilege, too—raised in a big house, without a shred of economic anxiety in any of its rooms.

A decade later, as Jewish philanthropy is still assessing the degree of disaster wrought by Bernard Madoff, a Jewish swindler of the highest order, surrounded by blinking warning signs throughout his investment-management career, we can see the foolishness of this kind of preference for Jews.

Madoff felt like a brother or a cousin; he was Jewish in affect and social identity. But he was a crook nonetheless. A Jew can be a dishonest business man, or a dishonest husband or wife. If our goal is to find a smart, trustworthy business partner, we should always look for direct evidence of good business practice, intelligence, and honor. Religious identity is silent on these matters.

If our goal is to find a good spouse—or a good son- or daughter-in-law—will the same not hold true? "Ah," I can hear a dozen aunts and uncles, great-aunts and grand uncles, saying, "*good* isn't the point; good isn't good enough. Yes, good is a requirement, but good *and* Jewish. That's what we're looking for."

This is another way of making clear that Jewish identity matters not because it is good in any absolute sense, but because it's good for the Jews as a people. My aunts and uncles don't merely want their children to be happy and good in their marriages—they explicitly want them to have Jewish children, for the sake of the Jewish people as a people. Jewish identity matters for the sake of the group, without regard for the morality of good and evil, on a separate set of terms. Jewishness itself is a distinct category of virtue, something good without regard to argument or evidence, an absolute.

If this is so—if Jewishness is an absolute good in its own right—then we ought to work to fill the world with more Jews. More Jews equal more Jewish identity, more good. But if we emphasize Jewish values and the Jewish experience of God—rather than Jewish identity as an absolute—then we may take comfort in the notion that if there is only a single Jew left, but a deeply good Jew who sees and feels the full depth of God's presence in the world, then Judaism is as strong and meaningful as it ever could be. This is the Judaism of virtue, the Judaism of feeling, of abstract religious experience, the unworldly side of a decidedly worldly religion.

■

The issue of Jewish virtue is far from simple, and it leads directly to the challenge of Jewish universalism. Those of us who take for granted the moral universalism of the Declaration of Independence, of Kant and Jefferson and King, resist the tribal certainties of the five books of Moses. We wish Judaism was a universal religion at its core, focused on the survival of all people and all souls. But the core texts tell a different story, one of a special people—a chosen people—and God's special concern for them. Still, Judaism has never been static; and as Jewish scripture grew beyond the five books of Moses, hints of moral universalism surfaced early on.

Philosopher Michael Walzer finds a bit of this universalism in the books of the Prophets—though he has to look hard for it. Like many Jews, Walzer wants to see in the foundational texts of Judaism the same kind of moral universalism that we take for granted as the political inheritance of the modern Western philosophical tradition. Yet the five books of Moses put the interests of the Jews at the center of Jewish morality and take a harsh stance toward, as examples, the Canaanites, Midianites, and the Amalekites, establishing a separate category of moral obligation toward the men, women, and children of these and other groups, at times flatly suspending any moral regard for them as fellow humans. But as Jewish teachings and tradition grew over the centuries, more and different teachings emerged. Walzer movingly quotes the eighth-century BCE prophet Amos:

*Are ye not as the children of the Ethiopians unto Me, O children
of Israel? saith the* LORD.

*Have not I brought up Israel out of the land of Egypt, and the
Philistines from Caphtor, and Aram from Kir?*

So while the five books of Moses offer a tribal kind of
virtue, Judaism is becoming at least a bit more cosmopolitan
and universal by the time the second ring of sacred Jewish
texts is written into the canon.

Walzer makes an important choice in stepping beyond the
core of the Torah, to the Prophets, to find a moment in the
evolution of Jewish morality in which the Other is elevated
and the universal moral value of human life is affirmed. Yes,
God loves the Jews, but he also loves the Philistines, he also
loves the Arameans. And these seem to be only the examples
closest at hand. The message here is that God loves all men
and women, and even the extraordinary story of Exodus is
not a gift that God gives to the Jews alone.

A similar choice was made by Rabbi Abraham Isaac
Kook, the chief rabbi for the Jews of Palestine under the Brit-
ish mandate. Writing at the close the nineteenth century, he
offered this striking commentary:

The Torah commands the Children of Israel to conquer the land
from the indigenous nations. But this is clearly unacceptable! How
could God, Whose mercy extends to all His creations, oppress His
own handiwork?! How could the Most High command that we
remove from our hearts the well being of the entire human race
for our own selfish good?! Therefore, at the time the covenant
was first established with our ancestor Abraham, a divine protest
was lodged: The very thought of nationalism is despicable to God,
for He equates all mankind. The goal is to seek the true success of

all God's creations. True justice means that one views with equal concern the advancement of the entire human race.

Kook's comment here comes from a larger discussion of *parashat Vayishlah,* from the section in Genesis in which Jacob wrestles with an angel and encounters his brother Eseau. That bit of scripture sets the stage for some of the most troubling judgment of some tribes—including those descended from Eseau—as "banned" and ultimately without any moral value or status. These become the nonhuman humans, the people exempt from God's concern; indeed, these people become the enemies of God. Certainly Kook knows this. All people are not created equal in the Torah—not equal in God's eyes and not equal before God's law.

But Kook does not accept this—cannot accept this. For him, there is an obvious moral truth to universalism. He takes a nontextual position—"This is clearly unacceptable"—and ends up declaring that we, mere men and women, must be reading the Torah wrong because this book is the divine map of the world and its truths, and therefore it could not violate the most obvious moral truths. Kook has a conflict: obviously God's equal love for all people is true, yet the Torah takes a different position. His resolution: we must be misreading the Torah.

Kook and Walzer offer two fascinating expressions of the Jewish desire for virtue over tribal strength: one drawing on the evolving set of Jewish texts; the other, on the kind of self-evident morality that drives the humanism of the Enlightenment. But theirs are clearly not the only positions. Extremist political and religious leader Meir Kehane put his own view starkly. "THE JEWISH PEOPLE IS UNLIKE ANY OTHER," he wrote in "The Authentic Jewish Idea." He continued, "It is a Divine, special, holy and different nation, chosen by the

All-Mighty at Sinai to live a specific life under Jewish law and commandments. Jewish destiny—that which will be—depends on one thing only: Jewish adherence to their special mission of obedience to that Law." This Judaism is protected by a theological border: the commitment of chosenness, the notion of a holy people that Kahane takes directly from Exodus. Kahane is roundly rejected by most Jewish leaders today, but his articulation of the special status of Jews is largely consistent with the core teachings of the five books of Moses.

We must decide. Are we to embrace the special status of Jews as a "people unlike any other," which is to say, with a special moral status? Or are we to make a universal human worth the center of our notion of how to live good lives? If the former, we will be better able to focus on the pragmatic strength of the Jewish people. We will be able to ask at every turn, "Is it good for the Jews?" and to use that question to map our way through the coming decades.

Or we can ask more simply, "Is it good?" and embrace the virtue of universalism—to be equally concerned with every life and to feel that we are most fully and deeply Jewish not when we protect and preserve the Jewish people but when we protect and preserve all of humanity, the weakest and most needful first.

"It's Not Always about Us"

One congregant at a New York synagogue tells me:

My real problem with the focus on what's good for the Jews is that it feels like the real function of religion—to get beyond myself and focus on something bigger, to make sacrifices in order to be part of a bigger spiritual world—is undercut by the narrowness of concern I hear often about Jewish issues. I just want to say, "It's not always about us." I want a Judaism that is more about sacrifice and less about what's in it for us. I don't care if my daughter marries a Jew and makes more Jews so much as I care that she marries a good man and makes good and decent children. I want to feel that what we do together as Jews is less about us—less about the population of Jews, about the strength of Jews—and more about doing good.

Of course, this invites a special kind of risk. By pulling down this theological border, we risk blurring the line between Jews and non-Jews, even as we all stand on a social and civic platform that tilts heavily toward a Christian norm.

It would be a relief to find other kinds of boundaries or points of difference that make moral as well as tribal sense. The Reconstructionist movement's emphasis on Jewish civilization offers the compelling vision of Judaism as tradition, as culture, as philosophy—everything a people does, except see and feel God. The great irony of Reconstructionist Judaism, though, is that it has grown in the decades since the 1930s to become so much more distinctly religious and God focused. Yet the reasons for this are clear enough. Kaplan and his generation of American Jewish leaders were mostly born in Europe, or to parents born in Europe. The insight that "in Europe, we went to shul *because* we were Jewish, while in American we go to shul *in order* to be Jewish" makes the point: Kaplan and his neighbors, his Jewish Theological Seminary colleagues, his family, and his congregation were so obviously Jewish and unavoidably tied to the civilization of Judaism, its flavors and accents, its melodies and prayers, its accomplishments and sufferings, that the question of Jewish continuity might have seemed absurd as Kaplan was writing his major works in the early 1930s. Europe was becoming a question mark for the Jewish people, but a glance around New York or Philadelphia or Baltimore or Chicago revealed Jews, Jewish culture, and Jewish worship deepening their roots.

In my family, both my wife and I can point to thoroughly secular family elders (my grandfather, her father) who legally changed their names to appear less Jewish when looking for jobs. The obvious fact of their Judaism—even though neither went to shul or took Jewish worship seriously—was inescapable for them. Neither would say that his name change was an effort to escape Jewish identity or continuity at all. Matters were more practical: they changed their names to more easily get work and to avoid blatant persecution outside their Jewish families and Jewish neighborhoods. But their personal identification as Jews was always explicit: they *were* Jewish.

If this was an essential fact for the large majority of American Jews in the 1930s, it was slightly less so for my parents and clearly less so for me. For my children, the tables have certainly turned. By doing nothing at all, my grandfather was nevertheless Jewish through and through. He lived among Jews, spoke Yiddish, and smelled like herring and pickles. My grandfather and father-in-law had to take action to be one degree less Jewish; passivity enforced their Jewishness. In contrast, if my children do nothing, they will become generic Americans, home for their schools' Christmas holidays, unless they opt to go off to build houses on their public school–sponsored service trips with Habitat for Humanity (a wonderful, widely beloved home-building charity that remains true to its founding as a Christian ministry). The border between Jewish and not Jewish is visible for them only with some effort. Similarly, the religious centers of Reconstructionism and Reform have become stronger as the observable *yiddishkeit* of young Jews has receded generation by generation. They do not minister to a population clearly and obviously Jewish; they must make the intentional embrace of Judaism an explicit part of their missions, or they will run out of Jews to bind together soon enough. They must point out the border between non-Jewish and Jewish to their congregants so that they remember—or come to know in the first place—that being a Jew means something specific.

But what is that specific something? If the oldest scriptures built the border between Jews and non-Jews principally through the idea of chosenness—and if we reject that as a proper center or boundary for our Jewish identity—then what are we left with? Covenant theology does not seem to work as it once did ("You're a Jew because Abraham made a covenant with God, and that's it, whether you like it or not"). Hearing a parent or a rabbi or a community leader tell a young person that he or she is a Jew and has no choice in that identity can sound like nonsense. It simply flies in the face of the feast of individual choice laid out before us.

For many young people, Judaism is a claim on them from outside their own lives and experiences—not all that different from the claim of Christianity through its universal moral sense. Where Christianity says to young Jews, "This religion is for you, because it is for everyone," Judaism says, "This religion is not for everyone, but it happens to be for you, because your mother is Jewish." The universal message of Christianity makes sense to young Jews of the West largely because that very message of Christian universalism undergirds the public institutions that shelter them. It speaks to the world we find ourselves in and to the moral principles we have absorbed by growing up and prospering in this world. Just as Rabbi Kook rejected the idea that God cares more about Jews than others because *this just can't be so*, the young people becoming the new generation of Jewish adults look at the literal claims of the five books of Moses and often say the same thing. But unlike Kook, they are not surrounded by millions of people pointing their fingers and yelling "Jew!" Kook was clearly and always a Jew regardless of his beliefs. Not so for most of our children today, particularly if the Jewishness of their mothers is not crisp and unassailable.

A Different Kind of Universalism

If we feel the urge to face a choice and choose both options— to keep Judaism as it has been and to make it new, to find a special status for the Jewish people and to find all people equally precious and close to God—there is, in fact, something Jewish about this impossible ideal. It begins with Abraham, the first Jew, who had it both ways more than once.

The twenty-second chapter of Genesis, which tells the story of the binding of Isaac as Abraham prepared to kill his son as a sacrifice to God, begins with a statement that pulls us back to the beginning of Genesis and lets us know that Abraham is a very different kind of man than Adam was. Like many chapters of the five books, it begins in the middle of a story, or stories, that have been unfolding in earlier chapters: "And it came to pass after these things," the text begins, "that God did prove Abraham, and said unto him: 'Abraham'; and he said: 'Here am I'" (Gen. 22:1). (Other translations say that God "tested," or "tempted" Abraham.)

Most important here is the exchange: God calls for Abraham, and Abraham says, in Hebrew, "Heneini" ("Here I am"). Earlier in Genesis, right after Adam and Eve had eaten the forbidden fruit, the text says that "God called unto the man, and said unto him: 'Where art thou?' And he said: 'I heard Thy voice in the garden, and I was afraid, because I was naked; and I hid myself'" (Gen. 3:9–10). Adam actually answers a question God has not asked him—and ignores the question that *was* asked. Instead of saying "Heneini," he scrambles, offering an excuse for his hiding—that he is naked. But in that excuse, he betrays the real cause for his fear of God—he has disobeyed—and only because of that disobedience has he come to know that he is naked. The sin is disobedience; and because of that sin, Adam no longer truly knows where he is. He cannot say, as Abraham does, "Here I am." The distance he has opened between himself and God is all that he needs to be utterly lost.

Abraham, on the other hand, hears God's question even when the text only hints at it—God "said unto him, 'Abraham.'" God only has to say his name, and Abraham understands what God is asking.

Beginning with that intimacy, the story proceeds with a series of doubles and paired choices from its very start:

And He said: "Take now thy son, thine only son, whom thou lovest, even Isaac, and get thee into the land of Moriah; and offer him there for a burnt-offering upon one of the mountains which I will tell thee of."

And Abraham rose early in the morning, and saddled his ass, and took two of his young men with him, and Isaac his son; and he cleaved the wood for the burnt-offering, and rose up, and went unto the place of which God had told him. (Gen. 22:2–3)

God's repetition—"thy son, thine only son"—emphasizes a claim that we know to be literally false: Abraham has another son, Ishmael, who has been cast out along with his mother, the servant Hagar. As Hagar wanders in the wilderness after being put out of Abraham's homestead, she places her son under a bush so that she will not have to bear watching him die. But he does not die. God comes to Hagar and creates a spring for her and Ishmael to drink from. God then tells Hagar that from her son a great nation shall rise, and indeed it does—Ishmael becomes the progenitor of Islam. Perhaps God tells Abraham that Isaac is his only son because Ishmael is no longer in his household, but there is clearly something larger at stake here. In one light, this repetition places Isaac in a special status that Ishmael will never have— clearly consistent with his exile from his father's house. Later, it will also be used by some to discredit Islam, whose lineage begins with a child God does not recognize.

The repetition, "thy son, thine only son," also leaves some commentators room over the centuries to wonder whether God is, in effect, splitting Isaac with this phrasing, making two of him, just as the very first chapter of Genesis tells the story of creation twice, creating Adam and Eve and then creating them again. One pair seems to be part of one creation story, with its own distinct tone and style; and the other, part of a different story, just as one Isaac perhaps perishes on the altar in one story of Abraham's fanaticism, while another lives and leads a generation of Jews, as part of a very different story.

This kind of analysis is beyond subtle—it can seem to pull more from the text than the text wants to give. But the doublings and pairings in the story of the binding of Isaac keep on coming. Two young men accompany Abraham and Isaac on the journey. Why? Abraham then cleaves the wood, again making two new pieces of wood ("cleaved" from one). The story continues:

And Isaac spoke unto Abraham his father, and said: "My father." And he said: "Here am I, my son." And he said: "Behold the fire and the wood; but where is the lamb for a burnt-offering?"

And Abraham said: "God will provide Himself the lamb for a burnt-offering, my son." So they went both of them together.

And they came to the place which God had told him of; and Abraham built the altar there, and laid the wood in order, and bound Isaac his son, and laid him on the altar, upon the wood.

And Abraham stretched forth his hand, and took the knife to slay his son.

And the angel of the LORD called unto him out of heaven, and said: "Abraham, Abraham." And he said: "Here am I." (Gen. 22:7–11)

There are two more instances of "Heneini" here: Isaac says "My father," and Abraham feels the question as fully as he felt the question in God's own uttering of his name. He responds with the same statement. He knows where he is, and he is not offering excuses for what he is about to do: "Here am I." And when the angel calls to stay Abraham's hand, the angel does not say his name once but twice: "Abraham, Abraham." One becomes two. But Abraham himself pulls the two back to one: "Here am I." His sense of his own presence and wholeness is complete.

Why does this matter? Because Abraham takes two distinct paths and makes them one—indeed, Abraham makes of Judaism a religion that is, at its heart, a uniting of contrary impulses. Abraham goes up Mount Moriah with God's voice in his ear saying the most impossible thing: you must kill your son. And like a prophet—or like a madman—he believes the voice. The full passion of faith is inside him, and he is willing to sacrifice everything. He goes up the mountain as a respected man, a leader, a man of means. If he comes down covered in blood, he will be something else entirely, for the rest of his life. He will step away from his conventional authority—he will become, in his society, the man who killed his son.

Abraham is entirely willing to be that new man, the prophet of blood instead of the more conventional man with faith and vision. But the angel stops him. Isaac is spared, and Abraham is as well. Now Abraham can be both men. He can be the prophet whose faith is absolute and unquestioning, who will cross any boundary of decency, convention, and blood to serve his God. And at the same time, he remains a man within the bounds of convention. He will not terrify his servants and his neighbors as he descends Mount Moriah. Abraham was tested, and he has passed. He has proven that he will pay any price the voice of God asks him to pay—and yet he has not paid it.

Abraham's precedent can be a troubling one. Be fanatical in your faith, some say, and God will save you from becoming a lunatic on the fringe of society. The implicit promise is there. You can rush the boundaries of normalcy in your religious passion and still be rewarded and respected as though you were a dues-paying member of the society of the plain and ordinary. You can have the passion and not pay its full price.

But Abraham's precedent can also be the most remarkable model of Judaism's potential for bringing together fundamental choices that seem mutually exclusive. "Abraham, Abraham" becomes a guide for a dilemma that we can hear as "Judaism, Judaism." We must, of course, make a choice between the Judaism of demography and the Judaism of faith. And yet, from these two Judaisms, perhaps we can make one, uniting them in a statement similar to Abraham's "Heneini."

Judaism could be like Adam and make excuses, not knowing where it is going or where it stands, all too aware of what it has done wrong, terrified by a future beyond the garden. Or Judaism could be like Abraham and listen for the voice of God, for that intimate connection that does not even ask of Judaism, "Where are you—where are you going," but instead is the sound of a breath, a question only half spoken but intimately understood. Yes, we are here. Yes, we are distracted by the world and its demands, but we listen first to the call of divinity.

Ecclesiastes, one of the Khetuvim, makes the same point, directly. A book that reads more like a collection of aphorisms than a story, Ecclesiastes sometimes feels like a catalogue of answers to every question asked elsewhere in the Jewish scriptures. Spoken by a wise man—sounding to me at times more like a great-uncle from the old country holding forth in Brooklyn than a prophet down from the mountain— Ecclesiastes never loses sight of God's presence. "The words of the wise are as goads," we are told: they get under the skin—they make us uncomfortable. But a sign of their wisdom is that they all point in the same direction. "As nails well fastened are those that are composed in collections"—that is, all alike in their strength and reliability—so the words of the wise "are given from one shepherd." The text continues:

And furthermore, my son, be admonished: of making many books there is no end; and much study is a weariness of the flesh.

The end of the matter, all having been heard: fear God, and keep His commandments; for this is the whole man.

For God shall bring every work into the judgment concerning every hidden thing, whether it be good or whether it be evil. (Eccles. 22:11–14)

The message is clear: Start with God; everything else will follow. We won't become better or make a better future by being like Adam. He thinks first of worldly things—noticing that he is naked—and is distracted from God's voice and meaning. We're much better off following Abraham's model instead. Abraham is a visionary *and* an ordinary man at the same time. He hears the voice of divinity, but that voice leads him back to practical concerns and ordinary life, though utterly changed.

The choice between two paths might be a choice, not of one or the other, but of which one first. And the story of Abraham offers an answer: first be filled with faith, however impractical that may seem, and then the practical will follow. Ecclesiastes agrees: God comes first and last. From God, you can find your way to anything else that matters. This might not make much practical sense, but the whole business of being a Jew does not make practical sense, as the economist pointed out. It is in the feeling of Jewishness that the future will unfold. Getting the feeling and the tone of Judaism right is the part of Judaism's challenge that we can address best, and should address first. We'll still wind up living in the world of the practical, where demographics matter; but we should first get enough of a glimpse of God's intention, presence, and power to understand, even as we count how many Jews there are, that the real game to be played is to be *good* Jews first and foremost, our goodness grounded in something beyond ourselves.

"We Must Become Broad-Minded"

While Judaism is matrilineal, Zoroastrianism hinges on the faith of the father, not the mother. One thought within Zoroastrian communities recently has been to reach out to children of non-Zoroastrian fathers. "We must become more broad-minded," the *Boston Globe* quotes a Zoroastrian priest in India as saying. "We must welcome children of mixed parents and maybe even some new converts into our community." But others disagree. One defender of the faith in Mumbai, sounding not entirely unlike a rabbinical judge with his genders reversed, replies that "purity is more important than numbers. Our religion is interwoven with our ethnicity [and] can only be passed on through a Zoroastrian father."

Even non-Zoroastrians are a little bit worried about the demographic slide of their neighbors in some areas. "[Zoroastrians] are a wonderful and mad lot," Jiten Gandhi, a Hindu stockbroker in Mumbai, told the *Globe*. He said that he "could not live without Parsi jokes or bakeries." The *Globe* notes that these Zoroastrian bakeries in Mumbai are part of the city's culture, celebrated for "grumpily serving patrons sweet tea and hot 'brunpau,' a crusty bread," echoing at least a little bit the pleasures of a good bagel on the Upper West Side of New York.

A 2007 report by the Religion News Service captured a few more voices in the continuing debate about the future of the Zoroastrians—a debate that pits self-styled orthodox Zoroastrians against their reformist brethren:

The orthodoxy treasures the rituals of the tradition and is dead set against interfaith marriage. Zoroastrians, they say, are born, not made.

Khojeste Mistree, an Oxford-educated community leader among the orthodoxy in India, talks about his concerns passionately with a twinge of fury and flabbergast. "You need someone to take a principled stand rather than a stance of convenience," he says.

The reformists, meanwhile, assert that their prophet Zarathushtra had a message open to everyone wanting to live "the good life" and it should not die out. They say the religion grew insular due to the circumstances of history, not because Zoroastrians were meant to be a closed clan.

"We have a responsibility here in North America," one Zoroastrian retiree in Illinois says, "to keep up the religion of the Zoroastrians and not to become extinct."

■

Zoroastrians actually played a vital part in helping Jews not become extinct at more than one early and dramatic juncture in Jewish history. The largest city in the world in the era before the five books of Moses were written was Babylon, sitting about fifty-five miles south of present-day Baghdad. Babylon became more than a city, though. Over a number of centuries, its leaders conquered large areas of the Middle East and beyond, including present-day Israel. The Temple of Solomon, the first great center of Jewish worship and learning in Jerusalem, was built around 960 BCE. Four of the five books of Moses were likely in circulation by then, and the fifth, Deuteronomy, would follow in about three hundred years. In 586 BCE, Babylon conquered the Kingdom of Judah, including Jerusalem. The Babylonians destroyed the temple, and a portion of the Jewish population was cast into exile in Babylon. Forty-seven years later, the Persian emperor Cyrus the Great conquered Babylon and allowed the Jews to return. Even more, he encouraged the reconstruction of the temple and, according to some scholars, even paid for a good deal of its cost. The book of Ezra—part of the Khetuvim, the third of the three sections of the Hebrew Bible—tells the story:

Now in the first year of Cyrus king of Persia, that the word of the LORD by the mouth of Jeremiah might be accomplished, the LORD stirred up the spirit of Cyrus king of Persia, that he made a proclamation throughout all his kingdom, and put it also in writing, saying:

"Thus saith Cyrus king of Persia: All the kingdoms of the earth hath the LORD, the God of heaven, given me; and He hath charged me to build Him a house in Jerusalem, which is in Judah.

Whosoever there is among you of all His people—his God be with him—let him go up to Jerusalem, which is in Judah, and build the house of the LORD, the God of Israel, He is the God who is in Jerusalem." (1:1–3)

Cyrus seems to be saying that his success is due to the God of the Jews, an unlikely comment but one that points to the mutual influence of Zoroastrianism and Judaism.

That influence only deepened as the next chapter of Persian and Jewish history unfolded. About a hundred years later, in 434 BCE, the Babylonians again marched into Judah. They were unsuccessful in capturing the land, as they sought to rebuild their empire, but took captive ten thousand Jews—tradesmen with valuable skills. These ten thousand Jews established yeshivas, synagogues, and other building blocks of Jewish life in Babylon; and when the Babylonians were finally able to reconquer Judah in 422 BCE and forced the rest of the Jews into exile in Babylon, they found a Jewish civilization already growing there. In fact, as Alexander the Great swept through Mesopotamia two generations later and the Jews of Babylon were once again allowed to return to Jerusalem, only about forty-two thousand made that choice. The rest, about 1 million, remained in Babylon, which was by then—and would remain for centuries—the greatest center of Jewish learning in the world.

Cyrus was the first great Persian emperor, and his kindness toward the Jews was decisive not only in the rebuilding of the temple in Jerusalem but also in the rich Jewish culture in Babylon that sustained the Jewish people through centuries of back-and-forth exile and general turmoil as empires clashed around them. Babylon was home for the Jews, and the monotheism of Zoroastrianism certainly borrowed from—and lent to—the evolving ideas of God at the heart of Judaism in a critical period for the writing and editing of the Hebrew scriptures.

Scholar Peter Clark, in his book *Zoroastrianism: An Introduction to an Ancient Faith*, has written that

the years of exile and those immediately following it formed what was in all likelihood the most significant period of theological activity in the entire history of Judaism. The exile had meant that the Jews were for the first time separated from their god, and so as their captivity continued they began to reconsider how they should understand him. Because it would be unthinkable to suggest that he had completely detached himself from them, the Jews began to view him in more universalist terms, ceasing to confine him to one geographic area, or one ethnic group.

The God that Jews arrived in Babylon with was a bit different from the God they eventually left with. The earlier Jewish God was a deity strongly associated with a place—Jerusalem—that the Jews no longer inhabited. "How can we sing the song of Yehwah in an alien land," the Psalmist sings in Psalm 137. The answer is that Yehwah will adapt to become the kind of God a man or woman can worship anywhere.

If the section of Ezra included above hints that Cyrus follows the path of the Jewish God, this is hardly an accident. Cyrus was certainly not Jewish, but where the God of the Jews ended and the god of the Zoroastrians began became less clear as Jewish civilization grew and thrived in Babylon. Even the rabbinic idea of healing the world—*tikkun olam*—which emerges in the Talmud and has become central to Reform and Reconstructionist Judaism, owes something to the Zoroastrian hymn in which the prophet Zarathustra is celebrated as the first of many prophets who will be born with that special mission, put in precisely the same terms: to heal the world.

Cyrus was emperor for thirty years. He died in 530 BCE and was followed by his son Cambyses II, who conquered Egypt. After Cambyses II came the reign of Darius—the Persian emperor celebrated in the Behistun Inscription. Darius continued the expansion of the Persian Empire and came close to conquering Greece, only a few generations away from its own golden age, before the Persian armies were stopped at the Battle of Marathon. With Egypt, Babylon, and Judah firmly in their control along with countless other smaller civilizations strewn across the Middle East—and Greece perhaps only a battle away from their grasp—the Persians and their Zoroastrian faith were the single most powerful force in Europe and Asia for centuries.

Today, their few remaining number own bakeries in Mumbai, populate at least one summer camp in New Jersey, and argue about the best ways to fight against their final demise and extinction.

And the Jews Too?

Hearing this as a Jew, I ask whether we—whether I—have a responsibility to fight against the extinction of my own religion. Yet even this word—extinction—makes me uncomfortable. It does not quite fit. Extinction is the language of biology, not of faith. The demographic end of the Jews—or the Zoroastrians or the Christians—would not, in fact, be an extinction but a change from one set of ideas to another. The Jewish people may cease to be Jewish, but they will not cease to exist as individuals. They will not *cease*. And in all likelihood, they will not cease to think about God—they will instead do so differently.

How do we shore up the Jewish kind of thinking about God that we hope will survive? We could all become like the aunt in my family selling Judaism to the children and boycotting their weddings if our salesmanship falters, but in the process we would destroy something precious. We make the unconditional love that is so often the very cliché of Jewish parenting dependent on a particular kind of Jewishness. Clearly this is the wrong path—it is victory at the cost of virtue. It is reaching out for new clothes, discovering that we are naked in our vulnerabilities. Like Adam, we know too much about too many new things in the practical world, and we have lost faith in the power of faith itself.

There is a better path, one that begins with the divine voice and our commitment to follow it. It seems like a mad path, as though we will cast aside all our practical needs in order to have a future—to make more Jewish babies, to have more Jewish neighborhoods and bagel shops and day schools. But this is the path that allows for faith to come first and for us as a people to be able to say, "Here we are."

The next photograph offers an indelible image of a number of men and women, Jews and gentiles alike, walking down that path.

March 21, 1965: John Lewis (D-GA), Ralph Abernathy, Martin Luther King Jr., Ralph Bunche, Abraham Joshua Heschel, and Fred Shuttlesworth, among others, on the Selma to Montgomery march.

CHAPTER FOUR

The Third Photograph

□   □   ■   □   □

About twenty years ago I stood in front of a gothic stone building at the corner of 114th Street and Broadway in New York City, Broadway Presbyterian Church. I was a graduate student writing a dissertation about Martin Luther King. My interest in King was specific: I wanted to understand how he had made so much political change in our country mostly by giving speeches.

My professors liked the topic. English departments at the time encouraged the idea that language might drive social change, and they especially liked anything hinting at revolutionary politics. The one thing that some professors were uncomfortable with, though, was the God talk woven throughout King's speeches and books. It snuck up on me as a student. I choose King as my subject because of what he had accomplished, without any particular interest in his religious ideas or commitments. But King's religious vision was at the center of everything he did, and I learned a tremendous amount about American Christian theology and church history as my studies unfolded.

At the same time, I was also hoping to find a rabbi. I'd had many surface points of resistance to my Jewish religion, but also a clear sense that underneath was something important that I wanted to be part of. So I temple shopped now and then, but I hadn't found a place or a person who felt like my way in.

I was explaining this to my friend Lisa from Mississippi, standing with her on that particular day on Broadway. She was a great friend, a very smart person, and someone I was beginning to think of as a source of humble wisdom in an environment filled with aggressive geniuses who don't actually know much. So I liked her and listened closely to her thoughts about my quest for a rabbi. I told her that maybe my problem was that I was looking for a rabbi like Martin Luther King—a lot to ask of a rabbi, no? "Well," she said, "why don't you come to our church this Sunday? It's right here"—she pointed behind her to Broadway Presbyterian. "You know," she added, "our minister, Pastor Rosenbloom, is also Jewish."

I was a little stunned by this. I'd been in and out of churches as part of my studies about King, and as a friend and neighbor, but never to seek my own salvation—and certainly not to seek my own rabbi. No, I told her, I just don't think I can. I can't go to church to look for what I'm trying to find.

I kept at the research on King, reading all the speeches, learning about what he studied in his years at Morehead College, Crozier Theological Seminary, and Boston University, exploring the African American church culture he grew up in and the Social Gospel movement he took up in his years at Crozier, regarded at the time as a white seminary in the mainstream of the Protestant theological world.

A relatively young minister and theology professor, Walter Rauschenbusch published a book, *Christianity and the Social Crisis*, that sparked the Social Gospel movement in

1908. It had enormous impact and inspired generations of Christian ministers to look out their church windows and act more intently to make social change in their communities. Rauschenbusch framed the problem as one of temptation: Protestant American churches at the beginning of the country's great century were close to the center of institutional power, and Rauschenbusch thought they were siding too often with the rich over the poor.

Instead, he urged, "Let us do our thinking on these great questions, not with our eyes fixed on our bank account, but with a wise outlook on the fields of the future and with the consciousness that the spirit of the Eternal is seeking to distil from our lives some essence of righteousness before they pass away."

King read the book, heard his professors lecture about the movement, and joined in the great tradition of the Social Gospel. Talk to professors of theology today about the best ways to understand how King did what he did, how he became Martin Luther King, and two answers emerge again and again: study the black church and study the Social Gospel movement.

When I took the book out of my university's library, blowing a fair coating of dust from its cover, I was stunned to find the first chapter focused on the Jews. "However our views of the Bible may change," Rauschenbusch wrote, "every religious man will continue to recognize that to the elect minds of the Jewish people God gave so vivid a consciousness of the divine will that, in its main tendencies at least, their life and thought carries a permanent authority for all who wish to know the higher right of God."

Seeing an unjust world in the America of his day, one growing less equal and less fair, Rauschenbusch pointed his fellow clergy to the Jewish prophets: "The prophets were the heralds of the fundamental truth that religion and ethics are inseparable, and that ethical conduct is the supreme and sufficient religious act. If that principle had been fully adopted in our religious life, it would have turned the full force of the religious impulse into the creation of right moral conduct and would have made the unchecked growth and accumulation of injustice impossible."

Certainly King had a similar thought in mind when he replied, in 1963, from the city jail in Birmingham, Alabama, to eight fellow clergy (the rabbi of Birmingham's Temple Emanu-El among them) who had questioned his right to be leading protests in their city, calling him an outsider. King wrote that,

I, along with several members of my staff, am here because I was invited here. I am here because I have organizational ties here. But more basically, I am in Birmingham because injustice is here. Just as the prophets of the eighth century B.C. left their villages and carried their "thus saith the Lord" far beyond the boundaries of their home towns, and just as the Apostle Paul left his village of Tarsus and carried the gospel of Jesus Christ to the far corners of the Greco Roman world, so am I compelled to carry the gospel of freedom beyond my own home town. Like Paul, I must constantly respond to the Macedonian call for aid.

It makes all the sense in the world for King to talk about the Christian apostle Paul, but to hear him say first that he is following the path of the Jewish prophets is a surprise. Less so, perhaps, with Rauschenbusch in mind. And less so if one reflects on the disproportionately large presence of Jewish volunteers in the civil rights movement, a fact that Jews across the world can be rightly proud of, but also a fact with complicated meanings and messages.

■

In the summer of 1964—a year after King's 1963 "Letter from a Birmingham Jail" and a year before the photo above was taken, of King and theologian Abraham Joshua Heschel—Jewish civil rights workers became international news.

The story that made so much news that summer began with two young men, one a Jewish northerner and the other a local African American, in an old station wagon driving down a small road toward a small church. At the small church, several dozen African American people were gathered for their Sunday service, with perhaps a few more congregants than usual in attendance, because it was Memorial Day. The young men were part of the Freedom Summer effort to register masses of African Americans in the Deep South to vote.

These young volunteers were clearly hated by the white establishment in Neshoba County, Mississippi, where the little church sits, in the hamlet of Longdale just outside the town of Philadelphia. They were hated by poor whites, too; by white men and women; by white children; even by some African Americans who understood the violence and loss that would inevitably be part of the struggle for the vote.

The hatred of these two men was rooted in a sophisticated understanding of what they represented, of the inevitable changes bearing down on this small town and on what many in it would have described as their way of life. These two young men in their station wagon driving down the road to the Mount Zion Methodist Church represented a movement in American history and culture that would have meant the end of much of the power of the feudal landowners and sheriffs in the places they ruled. They represented, as well, an end to the common understanding that white men would not go to jail for killing African American men or women.

After these two men—James Chaney, from Meridian, Mississippi, and Michael Schwerner from New York City—spoke at the church and left, services ended, and the congregation began to disperse. But as they drove off, departing churchgoers were pulled from their cars, beaten, and threatened by white men. A few days later, the church was burned to the ground. And a few days after that, when the two young civil rights workers returned with a third companion, Andrew Goodman, also from New York, also Jewish, to talk to witnesses of the burning, all three were first arrested, then released at night and driven off the road as they left town. Then they were killed and buried in an earthen dam.

The parents of Goodman and Schwerner enlisted their local congressmen to demand a federal investigation into the disappearance of their sons—something the family of a missing black activist would never have done, a fact made clear once the search for the missing three men began in earnest. The FBI and other federal law-enforcement agents dragged local swamps and found several bodies, all black, one still wearing a Congress of Racial Equality T-shirt, but not the three they were looking for. Those specific three were in the dam, not the swamp.

In December of 1964, nineteen men were arrested for the murders, all members of the Ku Klux Klan, including Neshoba County's Sheriff Lawrence Rainey and Deputy Sheriff Cecil Price. A U.S. commissioner in Mississippi—acting with the power of a local federal judge—dismissed the charges six days later. A federal grand jury reindicted the nineteen. Federal Judge William Cox then threw out the indictments against all but the sheriff and his deputy, but the U.S. Supreme Court reinstated them. Judge Cox then presided over the trial and sentenced the nineteen defendants to three to ten years apiece in federal prison.

Cox had been the roommate of arch-segregationist Mississippi U.S. senator James Eastland at the University of Mississippi. According to several sources Robert Kennedy was told by Eastland, "Tell your brother that if he will give me Harold Cox I will give him the nigger," referring to President Kennedy's impending nomination of Thurgood Marshall to the Supreme Court. Cox's rulings were often overturned on appeal, and he was not well regarded outside Mississippi. In fact, two northern senators, Javits of New York and Rodino of New Jersey, sought to have him impeached after he referred to a group of African American witnesses in a 1964 trial as "a bunch of chimpanzees." To court watchers from the South, the wonder of that incident was not what the judge said but that senators from the North cared.

And that was the very logic behind the appearance of Michael Schwerner and Andrew Goodman in Mississippi: making sure that the world cared. If the newspapers and their readers in New York and Chicago and Los Angeles and Washington DC did not think it news when a sheriff hunts down and kills an innocent black man in Mississippi, perhaps they would find more interest in that sheriff hunting down and killing a couple of young white men.

Rita Schwerner, wife of Michael, understood this. She told the press, "My husband, Michael Schwerner, did not die in vain. If he and Andrew Goodman had been Negroes, the world would have taken little notice of their deaths. After all, the slaying of a Negro in Mississippi is not news. It is only because my husband and Andrew Goodman were white that the national alarm had been sounded."

Brave though they were and complete as their sacrifices became, Goodman and Schwerner were not simple figures in the civil rights movement. The 1997 PBS documentary by Deborah Kaufman and Alan Snitow *Blacks and Jews* explored this issue. One woman, a veteran of the movement, told the camera, "Schwerner and Goodman, Goodman and Schwerner: I am so tired of hearing those boys' names. You'd think they was the only two ever strung up by the Klan." The echoing truth of this remark does not crowd out the truth of Rita Schwerner's comment. These two statements describe the same world, and even the same moral consciousness. Both wish for something better.

■

Many of the white men and women who went south in the spirit of sacrifice in those years of the civil rights movement were not Jewish, but a strikingly high proportion were.

The holocaust was still fresh in modern memory—barely fifteen years past. But that was hardly the only reason. A fundamental value of Judaism is tikkun olam, healing or repairing the world. Many—perhaps most—Jewish leaders are clear that this is a charge to make the world more just, a political in addition to a spiritual call to action.

Abraham Joshua Heschel certainly shared that belief. Born in Poland, Heschel emigrated to the United States in 1940. He had been arrested in Frankfurt in 1938, deported to Poland, and left for London only weeks before the German invasion of Poland. Many in his family, including two sisters, died in the camps. His mother died of a heart attack when the Gestapo came to the family's door.

In the United States, Heschel first taught at the seminary of the Reform movement and then settled into a long career at the Conservative movement's Jewish Theological Seminary, where he and Mordechai Kaplan were colleagues, though by many accounts were not friends, and were not fond of each other's work. To read their principal books is to understand why. Heschel focuses, always, on the spiritual—he never loses the possibility that the core Jewish texts say what they say because they are transcendently true. Kaplan, in contrast, grasps the Torah as a means to other ends. "The traditional Torah," he writes, "must be reinterpreted and reconstructed so that it becomes synonymous with the whole of a civilization necessary to civilize and humanize the individual."

The task of civilizing and humanizing the individual is the moral center of religious experience for Kaplan. To try to find the spiritual center of his work is challenging. His view is practical, ethical, cultural, and historical—but not clearly spiritual. The central Jewish texts are, for him, tools to reach virtuous outcomes. The voices emanating from the Torah don't speak to him but speak to "the individual," in a generic sense, and ought to be framed and managed just so, to have the most useful effects. Heschel, in contrast, hears the voices directly. "Prophecy," Heschel writes, "is a reminder that what obtains between God and man is not a contract but a covenant. Anterior to the covenant is love, the love of the fathers, and what obtains between God and Israel must be understood, not as a legal, but as a personal relationship, as participation, involvement, tension." Like Kaplan, he is speaking about the individual, but his individual is in close contact with a vibrant God. "God's life," he writes, "interacts with the life of the people. To live in the covenant is to partake of the fellowship of God and His people. Biblical religion is not what man does with his solitariness, but rather what man does with God's concern for all men." For Heschel, God is a powerful, elevating presence at the heart of Jewish experience—the center of a mystery that carries not only mankind but also the Torah to a level of divinity that we cannot fully comprehend but that we ought to strive to fully experience.

"Biblical religion" for Heschel is neither a tradition nor

a memory, but a living reality present all around him. His times are neither greater nor lesser than the times of the Bible—they are part and parcel of the fundamental, transcendental human moment. The biblical passions are our passions. The "participation, involvement, tension" are all with us now. The great struggles for justice and righteousness that we read in the Torah are here, now, if we raise our heads to see them. Prayer is where we make the connection between these eternal struggles and our own personal lives. Yet prayer is not about fulfilling commandments or rules, as it sometimes seems to be for those who emphasize the precise times, places, and order of prayers prayed in a blur of fast Hebrew just, one fears, to get it done, as the rules mandate. This is the prayer of obedience. Heschel wants something else.

"Prayer is meaningless," he writes, "unless it is subversive, unless it seeks to overthrow and to ruin the pyramids of callousness, hatred, opportunism, falsehoods. The liturgical movement must become a revolutionary movement, seeking to overthrow the forces that continue to destroy the promise, the hope, the vision." That spiritual logic is what leads him to King, and to Selma, where he'll march, praying, as he said, with his legs.

■

Taken on March 21, 1965, the photograph above pictures the third attempt by a group of marchers to cross the Edmund Pettus Bridge at the edge of Selma, Alabama, and walk on to the state capital, Montgomery. The first attempt took place on Sunday, March 7, when John Lewis (today a congressman from Atlanta) and Hosea Williams led a group of about six hundred protestors in a march to commemorate the killing of a young man several days earlier, shot by a state policeman as he shielded his mother during a protest.

Heschel and King look toward the camera, while the dozen other marchers clearly visible look in different directions. On the far right of the photograph, Fred Shuttlesworth—a celebrated Birmingham, Alabama, church leader—looks down and seems almost reserved in his stance; on the other side of the photograph, King's close colleague Ralph David Abernathy seems more at ease than the others. Abernathy is dressed in a workingman's hat and jacket in contrast to the formal coats and hats of King, Shuttlesworth, Heschel, and Ralph Bunche. He commands more space, and seems unaware of the camera as he holds the hand of the white nun on his right—a gesture that could land him in jail or worse, with or without the protest march. King and the three formally dressed men on his left cluster more closely together and loom a bit toward the camera. The men and women on King's right are more loosely assembled, seeming more at ease and less burdened by the moment. They are mostly free of the shadows that fall across the faces of Bunche, Heschel, and Shuttlesworth.

Even in this varied assortment of notable and colorful men and women, Heschel stands out. Hatless, wild-haired, and wearing a prophet's beard, he smiles. Only he and the nun, who is at the other end of the photograph and made smaller by the camera's angle, smile. Heschel's right hand is at the front of his dark coat, at the center of his body as he marches forward, arm in arm with the very formal looking Bunche and Shuttlesworth, his head darkened by shadow. The entire group, in fact, is about to step over the shadow of a pole or power line reaching across the front margin of the photograph. Heschel is the farthest forward, his stride is the broadest, and he more than any other figure across the line of marchers seems to understand that his steps are a message to the people who will one day look at this photograph and wonder what these men and women felt, feared, and hoped as they walked.

■

Two weeks earlier, a similar group of marchers had planned to walk from the Brown Chapel African Methodist Episcopal (AME) church in Selma to Montgomery over three days. They were dressed for cool weather and many carried backpacks and sleeping rolls. As they crossed the bridge leading out of Selma, a group of state police, some on horseback, bore down on the marchers, meeting the column with violence. Many were beaten; one died. John Lewis suffered a fractured skull.

That day, CBS was televising the first widely seen documentary about the Nazi assault on Jews and others in Germany, and the network cut away from the documentary to show scenes of police beating men and women dressed in their Sunday clothes attempting to walk across an American road. Some who saw the footage, at first, thought it must be a part of the documentary. Many viewers later recalled that as the CBS news commentary made clear that this was new history unfolding in *this* country, the connection between the violence of the Alabama state police and Germany's Nazis was inescapable.

Beaten and shocked by the violence, the protesters returned to the church. Across the country, millions who had witnessed the scene on television organized follow-on protests in their own communities. Some traveled to Selma to join the protesters at the Brown Chapel. Martin Luther King was among them; and upon his arrival, plans for a new march coalesced. King would lead a column of marchers back to the bridge on March 9.

Often in the days of civil rights protest in the 1950s and early 1960s, violence had its cinematic qualities, and newsmen stood ready to record it for publication and broadcast. But the violence was no less dangerous because of that, and the fear among the marchers as they prepared for their second attempt to walk out of Selma was paralyzing to some. King walked at the head of the column. As the front rank of marchers crossed over, they saw a line of state troopers standing across the road with billy clubs blocking their path. Some marchers braced themselves for another assault; others began thinking of where they could hide.

King stepped forward and asked Major Cloud, the leader of the state police contingent, if he might be permitted to pray. The Major agreed and King bent in prayer, joined by a small number of others. When he stood back up, the troopers fell back, after a moment, to the side of the road—clearing the path for the marchers.

King looked down the road; turned back toward the marchers, some of whom were stunned by what they later described as a miracle; and told the marchers to return to the church. The group turned and went back to Brown Chapel. They prayed and sang and began planning a third march. That march, two weeks later, carried on all the way to Montgomery, with Heschel marching part of the way with King.

Heschel returned to New York after participating in a relatively short stretch of the march. King stayed longer on that first day, but he too left to return to other business before the day was out. King returned, though, for the final leg of the march, and gave arguably his greatest speech, to the crowd of a few hundred gathered in front of the Alabama State House. The audience was almost all black, and the speech was thinly covered in the media. Virtually alone among all of King's recorded speeches and sermons, the Montgomery speech talks about the white man. "Our aim," King says, "must never be to defeat or humiliate the white man but to win his friendship and understanding. We must come to see that the end we seek is a society at peace with itself, a society that can live with its conscience. That will be a day not of the white man, not of the black man. That will be a day of man as man." Not black, not white. Not Jewish, not Christian. King was an African American leader shaping a movement that he hoped would transcend African American identity, just as he was a Christian leader seeking to make of his movement something beyond Christian identity. Can Judaism—should Judaism—strive for an ethical position that, similarly, points beyond Judaism?

■

Martin Luther King met Abraham Joshua Heschel on January 14, 1963, at a National Conference of Christians and Jews in Chicago. Heschel's speech at the event began this way: "At the first conference on religion and race, the main participants were Pharaoh and Moses. . . . The outcome of that summit meeting has not come to an end. Pharaoh is not ready to capitulate. The exodus began, but is far from having been completed. In fact, it was easier for the children of Israel to cross the Red Sea than for a Negro to cross certain university campuses."

Heschel was deeply engaged in the moral and material struggles of the civil rights movement. He rarely missed an opportunity to talk about the just cause and the great courage of marchers and protesters. The issue was more than social or political to Heschel. It went directly to his sense of connection to God and his role as a spiritual leader. In a telegram to President Kennedy, accepting an invitation to take part in a dialogue among clergy about race at the White

House, Heschel wrote that "We forfeit the right to worship God as long as we continue to humiliate Negroes."

After the second attempt to march across the Pettus Bridge in March of 1965, Heschel presented a petition to the regional head of the FBI in New York—at the head of a group of eight hundred protesters—condemning the brutality of Alabama state troopers and calling on the FBI to intervene. And then, following King's public call for clergy of good faith to join him in Selma, Heschel went south to march in the third, successful attempt to cross the bridge.

His daughter, the distinguished Dartmouth professor of religion Susannah Heschel, has written about his path to Selma and his experience there:

On Friday, March 19, two days before the Selma march was scheduled to begin, Heschel received a telegram from King, inviting him to join the marchers in Selma. Heschel flew to Selma from New York on Saturday night and was welcomed as one of the leaders into the front row of marchers, with King, Ralph Bunche, and Ralph Abernathy. Each of them wore flower leis, brought by Hawaiian delegates.

In an unpublished memoir he wrote upon returning from Selma, Heschel described the extreme hostility he encountered from whites in Alabama that week from the moment he arrived at the airport, and the kindness he was shown by Dr. King's assistants, particularly Rev. Andrew Young, who hovered over him during the march with great concern.

For both King and Heschel, the theological was intimately intertwined with the political and that conviction provided the basis of the spiritual affinity they felt for each other. Shortly after returning from the march, Heschel wrote to King: "The day we marched together out of Selma was a day of sanctification. That day I hope will never be past to me—that day will continue to be this day. . . . May I add that I have rarely in my life been privileged to hear a sermon as glorious as the one you delivered at the service in Selma prior to the march."

Toward the end of his life, Abraham Joshua Heschel gave a talk at Notre Dame University; and in the question and answer period following, he was asked about the anxieties of the Jewish people in a period of renewed Christian solidarity. Would Jews feel threatened by a stronger, more united Christian community? Heschel recalled the difficulties of his youth in Warsaw—being stoned by children as they left their churches—but ended on a note of optimism. "I take consolation," he said, "in the words of Jonahan Ha-Sandelar, a disciple of Rabbi Akiba, who said: 'Every community which is assembled for the sake of heaven will in the end endure; but one which is not for the sake of heaven will not endure in the end.'"

View the photo with this comment in mind, and the image of Heschel marching from Selma becomes a challenge about the future of the Jewish people: are we marching, today, where we should be marching? Are we living for the sake of heaven to enough of a degree that we will endure? Heschel is clear that only the goodness of our purpose as a people will give us a meaningful future. In this way, the third photograph answers the question of the first two—virtue and survival are not a pair of mutually exclusive alternatives, each depending entirely on the other.

■

There are other photographs of King with Heschel, but this photo is the most widely reproduced and the most meaningful, perhaps because in it they—two men among many others, all walking—echo the Jews in the desert, moving forward toward an ideal. They echo, as well, the prophets, going

from town to town, as King noted in his "Letter from a Birmingham Jail," with their "Thus saith the Lord." And notice
in the remark of Jonahan Ha-Sandelar the word "assemble."
There is a physical quality to an assembly—the ingathering
that is present in the march for justice, as King called on
clergy of goodwill across the country to gather in Selma and
to walk toward some better notion of a just society.

Heschel embraces the walk as a mode of prayer, a point he
explicitly made more than once—that he was praying with
his legs on that march. "Essential in prayer," he wrote in a
different context, "is the intention, not the technical skill. . . .
It makes no difference whether we stammer or are eloquent.
We can concentrate entirely on our own inner devotion."
And so there is a second challenge here from Heschel: are
we fully focused on our inner devotion as a people, or are we
too concerned with the "technical skills" of our lives—how
well we live in material terms, how strong and secure we are
politically and socially?

Heschel's message about the future is clear enough. We
must deserve a future in order to have one. We march to aid
our brothers, to heal the world, and to make ourselves wor-
thy of God's concern for man.

We heal the world because it is the one world we have. If
we allow it to be unjust—if we allow the bitterness of divi-
sion and domination to go unanswered by a Jewish voice—
then we have failed to testify to the higher possibilities of
humanity.

■

Heschel was talking to more than one audience when he
made his remarks about prayer and about justice. Certainly
he was speaking to the seminary students and Jewish scholars who followed his work and to a growing national audience that turned to him more and more often as a voice for

American Jews. But Heschel was also joining an argument, an argument with the Jews who say *this is not our fight* and *no good will come of this*—including Rabbi Milton Grafman, leader of Temple Emanu-El in Birmingham.

The letter that Rabbi Grafman signed along with seven other clergymen, admonishing King, appeared in the April 12, 1963, edition of the *Birmingham News* on the day King was jailed for violating a no-protest order signed by a local judge. "We are now confronted," the clergymen wrote,

by a series of demonstrations by some of our Negro citizens, directed and led in part by outsiders. We recognize the natural impatience of people who feel that their hopes are slow in being realized. But we are convinced that these demonstrations are unwise and untimely. . . .

. . . When rights are consistently denied, a cause should be pressed in the courts and in negotiations among local leaders, and not in the streets. We appeal to both our white and Negro citizenry to observe the principles of law and order and common sense.

Particularly sensitive to the charge of being an outsider, King responded in his "Letter from a Birmingham Jail":

I cannot sit idly by in Atlanta and not be concerned about what happens in Birmingham. Injustice anywhere is a threat to justice everywhere. . . . Never again can we afford to live with the narrow, provincial "outside agitator" idea. Anyone who lives inside the United States can never be considered an outsider anywhere within its bounds.

You deplore the demonstrations taking place in Birmingham. But your statement, I am sorry to say, fails to express a similar concern for the conditions that brought about the demonstrations. . . . It is unfortunate that demonstrations are taking place in Birmingham, but it is even more unfortunate that the city's white power structure left the Negro community with no alternative.

On a television show about her father, Susannah Heschel recalled a particular remark that he had made: "Hitler, he said, did not come to power with tanks and machine guns. Hitler came to power with words." King, Heschel thought, created a counterweight to evil with his words and through his protest marches. Heschel felt privileged to follow King's example.

Heschel knew that many Jews were embracing the civil rights movement because they recognized its inherent justice and because they heard in the treatment of America's African American population echoes of the treatment of Jews in Europe. But Heschel also knew that many Jews would not add their words and their feet to the movement because they feared that the movement would not be good for the Jews. It would risk the gains and the regard that Jews had established in the United States, particularly where those gains and that regard were most fragile, in the Deep South.

The death in 2009 of Helen Suzman, a Jewish antiapartheid activist in South Africa often criticized by the mainstream Jewish leaders in her country, occasioned this comment in the *Jewish Daily Forward*: "For decades, the SAJBD [South African Jewish Board of Deputies] maintained a cordial relationship with the apartheid government. Believing that Jews should not compromise their group interests by opposing the ruling powers, the board's leaders discouraged criticism of apartheid." Similarly, many American Jews worried for the relatively gentle berth they had found in this country.

Heschel spoke to those Jews. He called them to give up the practical calculation of short-term communal gain and to commit to the prophetic vision of justice. Cornel West noted in remembering Heschel that "his role was to be a prophetic figure, not just for the country, but for the Jewish people." His work was not merely to help heal the world, following tikkun olam, but to call the Jewish people to live, as he had said, for the sake of heaven—to do what is good even if the worldly cost is great.

■

Like most social movements, the civil rights movement had its share of rifts and fissures. After the enormous victories of the Civil Rights Act of 1964 and the Voting Rights Act of 1965, the movement lost much of its cohesiveness, and the perceived alliance of American Jews and African Americans in particular began its decline.

The Student Nonviolent Coordinating Committee was a group of mostly younger volunteers focused on the very dangerous work of registering voters in rural black areas of Mississippi and other southern states. In December of 1966, at a retreat in New York State, its members voted to exclude white people from active participation. Some participants in that meeting recalled, bitterly, the worldwide concern for Goodman and Schwerner while for so long so many thousands of local black men and women had been killed and forgotten. Many saw the expulsion as simply the next stage in a logical progression that began by putting white (and often Jewish) volunteers in harm's way for the sake of media and government attention, and then with that attention in place, turning away from whites as obvious outsiders.

And for a movement that had accomplished so much, yet for the moment lacked the feeling of momentum, there was an attractive intensity to the blacks-only faction. Stokley Carmichael's speech a few months earlier, during the March

1966 Meredith march in Mississippi, exemplified this view. Released from jail on a night when marchers were camping out at a black elementary school, Carmichael took to a podium and declared that he would not be going back to jail anymore—and then began calling out "Black Power," an angry chant that many of the gathered marchers were quick to take up.

I know that my own parents followed these developments with unusual interest. Young northerners with an infant child born in 1964, they felt a pull to go to the South but did not. My father was a teacher in a Brooklyn high school—a job he came to after a few years of unhappy work as an engineer, and one he cherished. Three years later, in 1967, the public school system in New York City set out to experiment with the ways that schools related to their local communities. An enormous system—today, New York spends more than $23 billion a year on schools—the city public education machine was rightly seen as a massive bureaucracy run by white people, largely disconnected from the many poor, minority communities it served. The stereotype of older white teachers sitting in their classrooms while young students of color sat across from them, separated by an unbridgeable divide, was often close to the truth.

A young aide to Mayor John Lindsay, Lew Feldstein, got a call one day to go to Lindsay's office to talk about a new project. "Lew," Feldstein recalls the mayor saying, "it's time to do something about the schools. See what's possible." A number of community groups and advocates for change in the city schools were already working through plans for trying out smaller administrative districts within the larger—indeed, massive—centralized school system, and Feldstein quickly identified this as the right path for experimentation. Feldstein worked with leaders of the Ford Foundation, who agreed to fund some of the extra costs of an experiment: taking three local areas and carving out self-governing mini school districts inside them. One of the three became the center of the storm that followed. That was Ocean Hill–Brownsville, a largely African American district in Brooklyn. There, Rhody McCoy, an African American veteran of the school system's administrative ranks, was assigned as the local superintendent. Community activists engaged in serious work planning for a new era in their local schools, which for decades had felt to many like white institutions stooping to serve their black children. Now they would change.

The new plan was launched in the beginning of the 1967–68 school year, the same year the local teachers' union led a citywide strike in September asking for, among other concessions, the right for teachers to expel disruptive pupils. Many African American parents and community members felt the demand was aimed specifically at children of color. A settlement was quickly reached, without giving teachers the new power to expel.

In May the locally staffed Ocean Hill–Brownsville school board ordered thirteen teachers, five assistant principals, and one principal to be reassigned, meaning that their jobs in the local district were terminated, though they remained school-system employees and would have to report to the central administrative offices of the city school system for eventual reassignment. All were white; a large majority, Jewish. They were identified by the Ocean Hill–Brownsville district leadership team as resisters and underminers of the various experiments in the district. Defenders of the reassigned faculty saw race and anti-Semitism as the central issues. White Jewish teachers were being pushed out of their jobs because of their identities, regardless of the quality of their work and their commitments to their students.

That very phrase—white Jewish teachers—captures one dimension of the politics of being Jewish at that moment. For a number of scholars and writers, the Ocean Hill–Brownsville controversy was the very moment that Jewish New Yorkers, and Jews in the United States generally, became effectively white, aligning for the first time with the culturally conservative Catholic, Irish, and Italian neighborhoods in New York against Mayor Lindsey and the larger agenda of social progressivism that he represented.

Many teachers—my father among them—found themselves facing a dilemma. This dilemma was especially vivid for teachers who were both Jewish and in any sense connected to the political left (and there were many of them—certainly this was the stereotype of the young New York City schoolteacher of the late 1960s).

The teachers' union in New York at the time was different from most teachers' unions in the county. For decades, a pair of small, squabbling unions fought red-baiting city and state agencies—abetted for a time by philosopher John Dewey—in trying to purge city schools of communist-leaning teachers. These unions, the Teachers Union and the Teachers Guild, lost most of their battles. In response, a more politically coherent—and radical—union arose in 1960: the United Federation of Teachers (UFT). The UFT was a strong and, at times, extreme voice for teachers. (In Woody Allen's dystopian fantasy film *Bananas*, the hero is revived a century after a nuclear holocaust has devastated the earth. How had it happened, he asked. "A man named Albert Shanker," he was told, "got hold of the bomb." Shanker was the head of the UFT.)

Teachers like my father, who was a strong supporter of the civil rights movement and had high hopes for the local strategy Lew Feldstein had helped to engineer, were faced with a choice when the union called its strikes over the course of an embattled year to protest the reassigning of the Ocean Hill–Brownsville teachers.

Would he express his political support for his fellow teachers and his bravely anti-McCarthyite union, or would he express his political support for the local district leaders and their vision of African American people guiding their own schools in their own communities? He'd rather have supported both if he could, but he chose to support the local leaders, and crossed the picket lines.

Over the course of the year, leaflets and pamphlets emerged from the extremes of both sides, at turns frankly anti-Semitic and blatantly racist, some purporting to be copies of the worst being circulated by the other side.

At the end of the year, the strike was settled in something of a draw. The teachers were given some concessions to strengthen their rights under local control, but the breaking up of the school system into more than thirty local districts began in earnest. My father returned to his regular classroom job after the strike. He was quietly told by his principal that because he had chosen the wrong side during the strike, he was no longer welcome on the faculty. He was eventually pushed out after daily observation sessions documenting every flaw, every day he taught. He was hardly the only one.

And he now thinks that he *was* on the wrong side of the fight. He remembers a radio show on the local independent public radio station, WBAI, in which a teacher got on the air and read a blatantly anti-Semitic poem, to the praise of the host. That show's host, the African American writer Julius Lester, later converted to Judaism and became a professor of Judaic Studies at the University of Massachusetts. Lester remembered the incident in his autobiography. On December 26, 1968, he had asked a black teacher from Ocean Hill–

Brownsville named Leslie Campbell to read a poem by a fourteen-year-old student. Campbell's response to Lester was simple: "Are you crazy?"

Lester remembers responding, "No. I think it's important for people to know the kinds of feelings being aroused in at least one black child because of what's happening in Ocean Hill–Brownsville." The poem began, "Hey, Jewboy, with that yarmulke on your head / You pale-faced Jew boy—I wish you were dead."

My father—whose memories of letters arriving in his Brooklyn apartment from relatives trying and failing to get out of Poland during the Holocaust are still vivid—is not moved by Lester's clarification. Having given up a great deal to support the leaders of Ocean Hill–Brownsville, he still feels betrayed and rejected by those for whom he sacrificed because he was a Jew.

Coming as the Black Power movement gained strength and visibility, following not long after the expulsion of whites from the Student Nonviolent Coordinating Committee, Ocean Hill–Brownsville led many Jews to feel that the seemingly natural—and precious—alliance between blacks and Jews was ruptured now beyond repair.

Twenty years later, I attended an academic gathering at Columbia University titled "Blacks and Jews in the Civil Rights Movement." About fifty people showed up, and seven or eight speakers sat in front of the room behind a long table. They each presented, and then questions began. Perhaps half the speakers were African American, all were academics of one sort or another, and most had played some role in the movement. In the audience, one black man—one of my professors—sat among an otherwise all-white and mostly Jewish assembly. During the Q&A, several audience members asked the kind of almost questions that felt more like manifestos. They included theories about why so few black people want to come out to events like this (most common theory: they're still busy struggling, while the Jews have enough relative prosperity and self-satisfaction to celebrate their heroic past). Many shared bittersweet memories of close calls outrunning sheriffs and Klansmen, and the camaraderie of jail cells filled with young civil rights workers.

Then an older woman rose to ask two questions: "Why are black people so quick to reject the whites and Jews who help them? Why do they bite the hand that feeds them?" The room immediately went silent. The figure of speech—thoughtless, I felt, but more than thoughtless—put African American people into the role of biting animals, with whites the noble souls bending to help. A bit nervously the conversation moved on, the question unanswered. The room never felt entirely comfortable, and the ideas expressed never got to the crux of the bittersweetness of some movement veterans and the absence of others.

■

As a trickle of early Holocaust documentaries and dramas played out on television in my childhood, my mother would make it clear that the lesson to take was that when there is trouble, flee. Be smart like the Jews who left in the 1920s and early '30s. Be like those who ran and lived—not those who stayed and died passively, and not those who stayed and fought either, because they died too. Fair enough as a message to a boy you hope will grow to old age, but that is not the message of tikkun olam.

My mother understood that in the face of overwhelming odds, the work of healing the world can easily lead to the demise of the healer.

Her position is entirely understandable; a mother seeks to protect her child. In some ways, it is similar to that of the Jewish people as a whole seeking to protect the next generations of Jews, our own children and grandchildren. We want them to live, to thrive, and to be good. But is that the correct order? When survival and virtue conflict, which should we tell them is more important?

Heschel's commitment to the civil rights movement was certainly driven by a commitment to virtue over survival; but because the movement was ultimately successful, it only enhanced the status of the Jews in the United States. Would his actions have had the same meaning had the movement faltered?

The practical importance of this question is great, because it leads directly to a larger concern: how much of the comfort and safety of Jewish people today is the right amount to risk to take up the moral causes that need champions? If Heschel had championed a losing cause with as strong—or stronger—a moral case as that of the civil rights movement and lost, would we look at him differently? For example, in 1829 an African American tailor in Baltimore named David Walker published a pamphlet, his *Appeal*, roundly criticizing Thomas Jefferson in particular and America in general for its horrific practice of slavery, noting the specific cruelties of this practice in a nation born out of a vision of individual liberty and human rights. He called on slaves to fight for their freedom. He distributed his pamphlet by sewing copies into the pockets and linings of the coats that black sailors left for him to repair while they were on shore. They would pick up their coats on the way back to their ships and then, eventually, find the pamphlets. Had Walker openly distributed his writings, he'd certainly have been killed.

Had the Jews of Baltimore risen up to carry the banner of his cause with Walker, what would have become of them? Certainly whatever tolerance and equality the Jews of nineteenth-century Baltimore enjoyed would have shattered. And, it is worth noting, the historical fact is that they did little to openly oppose slavery, as of course so few of any religion did at the time. Indeed, the abolitionist movement was—arguably—sustained as a movement largely of the well-off and socially respectable, because only they could manage to talk about these dangerous ideas openly, and even then only on occasion and in carefully chosen places.

Would we have called Heschel a fool for marching on behalf of *Walker's Appeal*, in a cause doomed to fail in its own time? Is there a reasonable degree of sacrifice and risk that we can calculate—go this far to help heal the world, but no farther—before we say, *enough*?

Philosopher Michael Walzer thinks so. Following his subtle and thoughtful discussions of just war philosophy over many years, he recently published an essay meant to clarify his idea of emergency ethics. There comes a point, he says, when a nation or a people will—and should—do almost anything to survive. Survive first, emergency ethics suggests, and then worry about being good.

There is a commonsense appeal to Walzer's idea of emergency ethics and a resonance as well with the tribal concern for the good of the Jews—above and beyond the good of other peoples—in the five books of Moses. *Of course* we should survive, most of us recognize. At the same time, though, we also recognize that even survival can come at too high a cost, George Barnard Shaw's question "What price, Salvation?" making the case. And so as Jews, we have to ask where our obligation to help heal the world stops and where our obligation to survive begins.

Shall we say that first *we* survive, and thrive, and then we help others? Shall we say that first we prosper, and provide for our children and our grandchildren, before we accept the risk of welcoming in the poor? Or is that too much? Shall we say that standing with the weakest in our work of marching and singing and calling for justice in the world is always more important than tending to our own practical interests? Sometimes? Never? Do we stay home from the march, from the occasion to pray with our feet, if the cost gets high enough?

Heschel offers an answer. Assemble for the sake of heaven. On earth we pay attention to what is good for us in practical terms. For the sake of heaven, we ask only "Is it good?" and not "Is it good for the Jews?" because Jewishness *is* an expression of goodness. From goodness done by Jews, the best kind of Jewishness follows. That is Heschel's standard; and if we are proud as Jews to see this man, so clearly one of our own leaders, marching with Dr. King, we must hear that question as we feel the pride: are we assembling for the sake of heaven today, or have we let other tasks, other dreams, or other fears keep us from that work?

From *Time* magazine:

This week ex-Nazi Eichmann goes on trial charged with arranging the murder of 6,000,000 Jews during World War II. Each day, for months on end, he will be led down a guarded back stairway to take his seat in the bulletproof glass cage that surrounds the defendant's chair, listening through a headset, speaking through a microphone. At Eichmann's left will be the three Israeli judges who will decide his fate. In the amphitheater at his right will be the world's press, TV and radio correspondents.

CHAPTER FIVE

The Fourth Photograph

□   □   □   ■   □

Adolph Eichmann was a Nazi officer who rose to the rank of lieutenant colonel in Hitler's army, though the rank seems modest given his later notoriety and the impact of his work. His task—largely completed—was to move millions of Jewish people (and a smaller number of others) from their homes to the death camps where most would perish.

Following the end of the war, Eichmann slipped out of Germany with forged Red Cross transit papers and made his way to Argentina, where he worked as a foreman at a Mercedes factory. In 1960, Israeli agents captured him, took him to a "safe house," interrogated him, and then smuggled him out of Argentina to Israel where he was put on trial for crimes against humanity and crimes against the Jewish people. At the end of his year-long trial, Eichmann was convicted by a three-judge panel and sentenced to death. He remains the only person to suffer the death penalty following conviction in a nonmilitary court in the history of Israel.

The photo at left captures the court where Eichmann was tried—a newly opened building, *Bet Ha'am*, the House of the People. The photograph's composition reinforces the feeling of bureaucracy on display here, the event itself holding the center of the frame, each visible individual quite small, each playing one role among many, the spectators in particular rendered tiny and almost indistinct. The room has been clearly built as a traditional theater, the camera looking on from the balcony. A man wearing a hat on the right of the stage—most likely a soldier or security guard—even seems to be leaning up against a wall, his hands behind his back, his face turned toward the judges and the judged. Two clichés join in this man: the civil servant passing time and the Jew (how many in his family were lost?) riveted by the prospect of justice. Or if not justice, punishment.

Eichmann stands before a microphone in a small, bullet-proof pen on the left side of the stage, two guards sharing the booth with him. The judges and their aides sit at the elevated bench, the stage upon the stage, under a small pendant hung high above them, the only decoration on any wall in the otherwise stark environment, showing the image of a menorah. The lawyers, both defense and prosecution, sit at tables just in front of the wide low-rise wall between the working elements of the trial and the spectators, who sit behind the wall, several steps below the stage. Several of the spectators, the camera catching the backs of their heads, sit bareheaded. Some might be women. One, certainly, is a particular woman with a circle of dark hair, the political philosopher Hannah Arendt, who wrote about the Eichmann trial for the *New Yorker* magazine and later collected her account in the book *Eichmann in Jerusalem*. The subtitle of that book—*A Report on the Banality of Evil*—proved essential to Arendt's argument and to the book's reception.

Arendt presented the trial of Eichmann as a national event. Israel, a nation barely thirteen years old and filled with survivors of the Holocaust, cared deeply about this man who had run the railroads carrying Polish and Hungarian Jews to death camps. Even as the war was ending, Eichmann made enormous efforts to send more and more Jews to the camps in the last possible moments. Many spectators at the trial had lost mothers and fathers, sons and daughters to the camps.

On many days, crowds gathered outside the courthouse to yell for Eichmann's death. Arendt wrote that Eichmann became the embodiment of *all* Nazis, the concentrated essence of the National Socialist moral monstrosity. A review in the journal *Human Rights and Human Welfare* of a 2005 book by Harry Mulisch about the trial and its coverage in the press captures the spirit of the moment:

France Soir, a French daily, declared [Eichmann] had "snake eyes," while *Libération* remarked that "each of his eyes is a gas chamber." A Dutch newspaper recounted the words of a popular minister: "Eichmann . . . has become a non-man, a phenomenon of absolute godlessness and non-humanness." Either paraphrasing or quoting Gideon Hausner, attorney general for the State of Israel and chief prosecutor, Mulisch writes that "it is no longer possible to believe in God; now let it at least be possible to believe in the Devil." . . . Hausner at the very least wanted to prove that Eichmann was "worse than Hitler."

And yet Hannah Arendt wrote, Eichmann was not a monster, not a freak, and not a man apart to any degree at all. She argues that he was instead strikingly similar to the ordinary people who walk the streets of any city in any nation in the modern world. His failure was to be all too ordinary. He did what he did because he was a conformist, a man demonstrating the qualities of likeability and respect for authority that in most places, at most times, help men get ahead and make them respected members of society.

Eichmann did not say no to his superiors. He did not

question the larger institutions and communities he was a part of. He worked diligently to perform his duties and to help those who worked under him accomplish their tasks with the greatest possible efficiency. He was, in a sense, the Nazi in the gray flannel suit—a thoughtless, modestly cheerful conformist.

"Despite all efforts of the prosecution," Arendt wrote, "everybody could see that this man was not a 'monster,' but it was difficult indeed not to suspect that he was a clown. . . . The judges were right when they finally told the accused that all he had said was 'empty talk,'—except that they thought the emptiness was feigned, and that the accused wished to cover up other thoughts which, though hideous, were not empty." Arendt argues the opposite: he was empty in the specific manner of the functionary, the booster of organizations, the too-loyal citizen.

With this portrait, Arendt completely rejects the moral judgment of Eichmann among the Israeli public. By labeling Eichmann a moral monster, Israel's press and political leadership established the first part of a two-part drama: to isolate and capture all that is evil. The second step is to destroy it. But Arendt understands Eichmann's significance in different terms. She links what's wrong with Eichmann to what's wrong with everyone, including Jews, and especially conformist, institution-minded Jews. She particularly goes after the leaders of the *Judenrate*, the official leadership organizations of the Jewish communities throughout German-controlled Europe, empowered by the Nazis to exercise a bit of control over the ghettos. These bodies were called on to provide lists of Jews, to keep order on the Nazis' behalf, and on occasion to organize the assembly of those scheduled for deportation to the camps. The leaders of these groups, Arendt wrote, were the very essence of bureaucratic morality—always compromising with evil, giving up their claims on decency inch by inch, heads held high all the while.

Writer Rich Cohen describes the typical emergence of one of the councils in the Jewish ghetto in Vilna, Lithuania.

Soon after the conquest of Vilna, [local Nazi commander] Murer appointed a Jewish Council to govern. The Council occupied the biggest home in the ghetto, a four-story brick building set around a courtyard just inside the ghetto gate. As members of the Council, Murer chose some fifty ordinary Jews: teachers, doctors, electricians, construction workers, engineers. . . . Murer also created a Jewish police force to keep order in the ghetto. He named Jacob Gens, a smart, officious forty-year-old, as chief of police. . . . He was the essence of the modern European gentleman. Gens built his police force of young men, Jews who saw in the force a way to gain privilege, to live outside the [racial] laws. The police wore white armbands with a blue Star of David. They stood at the ghetto gate as the sun rose, checking work permits of men filing out to the factories. Each night, they conducted searches and enforced curfews.

The light Arendt chose to shine on this kind of complicity was not particularly welcome among the Jewish public in the early 1960s. Some who by then held important positions in Jewish organizations—including in the Israeli government and in groups constituted to funnel reparations from Germany and other collaborator nations to survivors—were the very same people who had run the Judenrate. In a new age of organization, institutionalization, and bureaucracy in the Jewish world, a critique of the Jewish nation's collective outrage against Eichmann that culminated in a warning against the insidious effects of institutional power and social cohesiveness was bound to make enemies, and it did. Passionate criticism of Arendt continues today. Many readers glanced up from her reports in the *New Yorker* in bafflement—building off Eichmann's confessions and bureaucratic character, *she's blaming the Jews?*

The problem, as Arendt saw it, centered around the ability and habit of the individual—every individual—to think and reflect on his or her actions. "Clichés, stock phrases, adherences to conventional, standardized codes of expression and conduct," she wrote later in *The Life of the Mind* (an extended philosophical footnote to the much shorter *Eichmann in Jerusalem*), "have the socially recognized function of protecting us against reality, that is, against the claim on our thinking attention that all events and facts make by virtue of their existence. If we were responsive to this claim all the time, we would soon be exhausted; Eichmann differed from the rest of us only in that he clearly knew of no such claim at all."

Eichmann didn't think. Instead, he relied on the thoughts of the larger society around him, collected in clichés and prejudices, in easy opinions that would arouse little opposition because they arouse little thought—in fact, no thought at all, according to Arendt. Eichmann lived to follow orders, to be part of something larger than himself, and to find meaning in the symbols, actions, and stated needs of organizations that stood above him. He seemed grateful to be released from the burden of thought.

And this impulse to go along, to think less rather than more, Arendt tells her readers, is always with us. The symbols and actions and needs of a larger cause, or a larger group, are the very essence of nationalism, whether secular or religious. And now, in the new world emerging from the ashes of Europe, the Jews would have both kinds.

■

Before death camps became the preferred solution to the Jewish Problem, Zionists in Palestine often understood the benefits to their own cause of the earlier Nazi approach, expulsion. A steady stream of German Jews, often with some funds and useful skills, made their way to the settlements in what would become Israel. Eichmann, before he ran the railroads, was considered something of a specialist in Jewish issues and certainly thought himself a friend of the Jews. Strikingly, some Jews seemed to agree.

Scholar Francis Nicosia recently offered a well-documented account of a visit that Eichmann made to Palestine in 1937, to meet with a leader of the Hagannah underground Jewish militia (her book *Zionism and Anti-Semitism in Nazi Germany*, published by Cambridge University Press in 2008, is packed with unexpected detail). Eichmann arrived in Haifa on October 2, with plans to meet with Labor Zionist and Hagannah leader Feivel Polkes. Within a few days, Eichmann was expelled from the British-controlled territory. His papers listing him as an editor and his traveling companion as a student were transparent lies. Polkes met them in Egypt and agreed to funnel information to Eichmann in Germany in exchange for the Nazis allowing expelled Jews to exit with more currency if headed to Palestine.

Eichmann's later dealings with Zionists became the subject of a tape-recorded discussion he made while living in hiding in Argentina. *Life* magazine published excerpts from that tape in November and December of 1960. "I admired their desperate will to live," Eichmann said of the Jews in Palestine, "the more so since I was myself an idealist. In the years that followed I often said to Jews with whom I had dealings that, had I been a Jew, I would have been a fanatical

Zionist. I could not imagine being anything else. In fact, I would have been the most ardent Zionist imaginable."

About Reszo Kasztner, a Hungarian Zionist leader, Eichmann said that "He agreed to help keep the Jews from resisting deportation—and even keep order in the collection camps—if I would close my eyes and let a few hundred or a few thousand young Jews emigrate illegally to Palestine. It was a good bargain. For keeping order in the camps, the price of 15,000 or 20,000 Jews—in the end there may have been more—was not too high for me. And because Kasztner rendered us a great service by helping keep the deportation camps peaceful, I would let his groups escape."

And Eichmann was no aberration. Many people are shocked to discover that an official Nazi agency existed to encourage the Zionist mission. The logic was clear enough: both movements wanted Jews to leave Germany in greater numbers, at a faster pace. They shared this much at least in terms of their bureaucratic aims. The Zionist vision—even if motivated by love of the Jewish people—led toward the same short- and middle-term aims that the Nazi movement embraced at least for a time, even though the Nazis were motivated by hatred. The motives did not matter at all to those bureaucrats, those movement leaders, who chose to put aside the moral and ethical character of those they did business with. And this was Arendt's point: *of course* the bureaucrat does not reflect on the love and hate, the morals and ethics, bound up in his actions—that's what makes him a bureaucrat. And of course the movement leader makes deals with the devil. This is precisely the leadership question facing the statesman and political leader in times of crisis, everywhere from ancient Egypt to modern Israel.

Arendt's view of Eichmann surprised most of her readers and certainly stood alone among the flood of articles about the trial in Israel. *Time* magazine, noting the press section in the courtroom, explained that, in contrast to the general Israeli public, the assembled world press was "the more important audience, for Eichmann's guilt already was clear; the real purpose of the trial was to fix forever in the mind of the world the monstrous wartime crimes of the Nazis."

Arendt suggested that the real purpose might have been more complex. The purging of evil was as much the point as the display of horror, in her view. But her idea of evil was a distinctive one, and in some ways *Eichmann in Jerusalem* was a case study in the view of good and evil that Arendt had long embraced—a view that originated with a Christian saint, Augustine. His central idea about evil was that it was not an active presence, something foreign that had to be purged from the soul or society, but instead was an absence, the absence of good. From Augustine's perspective, then, the best way to deal with evil was not to kill it—because there was really no "it" to kill—but to fill the empty space that evil is, with goodness and love. Arendt wrote her PhD thesis in Germany, before the war, on Augustine's idea of love, and her book on Eichmann was in some ways a companion volume: the portrait of evil as an absence of critical thinking, individual character, and intellectual substance. Make these qualities real in a culture, she suggests, and they will displace evil. Encourage complex, reflective public discourse, and fascism will have a much harder time taking root.

Yet the discussion of Eichmann in Israel was anything but nuanced and reflective. The mob outside the courthouse called for his blood, and the political parties, the press, and the growing intellectual class in Israel largely concurred. Eichmann was convicted and killed in the name of humanity and in the name of the Jewish people. Arendt did not shed a tear for Eichmann, but she worried for Israel and for every observer coming away from the spectacle with a sense that the world was less dangerous with one less Nazi abroad, because she understood Nazism to be the work of ideas always at hand, at least to the same degree that it was the work of a debased group of soldiers and political leaders.

Her book was a warning about the nature of states and the nature of individuals. People are always tempted toward conformity and toward the kind of thoughtlessness that groups, movements, and nations thrive on. We pray for peace *here* but then go and prosecute war *there*. Perhaps any of us will need to make a compromise that we find ugly to serve a greater good, but let us at least be aware of the compromise we make, as Eichmann was not.

Just as the Judenrate required, to a degree, the suspension of ordinary ethical reflection among their followers, any state—including the Jewish state—will make similar demands on its citizens, most especially in times of crisis. When a state is threatened, the claims on its citizens' loyalty will be great—even when loyalty blinds the individual to the merits of his or her own country's position.

Arendt believed passionately that the problem of Nazism was not the presence of a malicious group of morally extreme individuals, but was instead the system of conformity within Germany that drove criticism and self-reflection out of the public spaces of the culture. And she saw similar traits on display in the reaction among other nations, including Israel, to Eichmann's trial. To guard against Nazism, she thought, we should police our own hearts and souls—and our own understanding of public virtue and national honor—and be alert to the kind of horrific simplifications and blind loyalties that drove the National Socialists. And so the virtues of group loyalty, of peoplehood and solidarity that many would suggest are vital to the survival and strength of the Jewish people, Arendt sees as dangerous in unexpected ways. Her test is clear: to what degree do these habits encourage the individual to think independently?

I had an experience as a teacher, in 1994, that illustrated to me exactly what Arendt meant by independent thought. I was teaching a university class called Writing about Crime and Violence. One spring morning, I picked up the newspaper and read about the killings of 29 Muslims while in prayer and the wounding of about 150 others, at the Cave of the Patriarchs, in the West Bank city of Hebron. Baruch Goldstein, a citizen of Israel who had grown up in Brooklyn, had walked into the cave that morning, carrying an automatic weapon and wearing his reserve officer's uniform. He passed a number of guards, stood in the main prayer area of the mosque, and opened fire. He was subdued by a group of men inside the cave, and then beaten to death.

We had been talking in earlier class meetings about when we should hold a government responsible for violence done by its citizens (Is the violence carried out by soldiers in the government's army? Is it carried out using weapons provided by the government? Is it carried out under orders?) as well as about definitions of terrorism (Does the act create terror in a civilian population? Does it turn seemingly safe places, part of community life, into places of deadly threat? Is it carried out without warning? Does it target civilians?). I reminded my students of these questions and then shared copies of the newspaper article. I was not certain—and I'm still not certain—whether we should define the killings by Baruch Goldstein as state action or as terrorism or as both. The writing style of the article I shared—from the *New York Times*—lacked moral judgment, but its just-the-facts approach allowed the horror of the killings to resonate. I wanted to talk about that.

One young woman, reading the article, connected the dots—she understood that we were going to talk about this horrible event and to ask questions that would consider culpability. She understood that we would explore the experience from many perspectives—perpetrator, victim, bystander, others. That's what we did in this class. She figured this out in a flash; lifted her head from the article; said, "I can't believe you're doing this. I just can't believe this," and left the room.

She didn't come back that day, and when we later spoke, she was angry. Israel was threatened by its neighbors, by some of its own citizens, and this was no matter for classroom analysis, she said. It was too close to her, too important for her family and her sense of community, and she simply refused to talk about it in the ways that I wanted to talk about it.

This, I think, is what Arendt was talking about when she pointed to reflective thought as the essence of public morality. If our allegiances prevent us from talking—or even thinking—about the possibility that our actions (individual or collective) might violate our most important ethical standards, then we are doomed to see practical interest and materialism of all kinds overwhelm our principles and our souls. We will become hardier survivors—but surviving *as what*?

■

Arendt's fundamental point about Eichmann's failures as a human being—that he was not a monster but a functionary, not different in direction or kind from ordinary people but different only in degree and in circumstance—holds a frightening challenge for Jews as we consider the role of Israel, the Jewish state, in the future of the Jewish people. Arendt suggests that any state, including Israel, will demand the kinds of things that all states demand of their bureaucracy—obedience, efficiency, commitment to the cause. And she suggests that these virtues, carried to an extreme, can lead to the kind of behavior that Eichmann exemplified. One does not have to look far to find Israelis who seem to agree.

Ari Shavit is an Israeli writer. Today, he is a visible columnist for the left-center daily newspaper *Ha'Aretz*. In 1991 he published an essay that appeared, in English translation, in the *New York Review of Books* as "On Gaza Beach." In it, he describes his recent tour on active duty as an Israeli Defense Forces reservist, guarding prisoners at a compound in Gaza. "The unjust analogy with those other camps of fifty years ago won't go away," he writes. It is not suggested by anti-Israeli propaganda. It is in the language the soldiers use as a matter of course: when A gets up to do guard duty in the interrogation section, he says, "I'm off, late for the Inquisition."

And N, who has strong right-wing views, grumbles for anyone who will listen that the place resembles a concentration camp.

M, with a thin smile, explains that he has accumulated so many days in reserve duty during the intifada that soon they will promote him to a senior Gestapo official.

There is no shortage of precedent in Jewish tradition for the dark side of governing and exercising force. In the book of Numbers, in the passage called Matot, just before the assembled Jews are about to cross the River Jordan and enter the Promised Land after their forty years of wandering, Moses calls together the leaders of the twelve tribes and asks them to each contribute a thousand soldiers to a force that will raid the nearby settlement of Midian. Earlier, women from Midian had come to the Jewish encampment, and some had slept with Jewish men and then encouraged them to worship the Midianites' idols. Twenty-four thousand Jews died in the plague that followed, as punishment for the transgression. The raiding party goes off to Midian and returns. The men of Midian have all been killed, the soldiers report to Moses. Tens of thousands of their animals and an enormous assortment of their household goods have been claimed as spoils. The women and children are captive, to become slaves. "You didn't kill the women?" Moses asks. No, they didn't kill the women. Then go now, Moses says, and kill all the women who are not virgins and all the male children.

Later, after they've had the chance to count up the returning soldiers, the commanders of the Jewish forces approach the priests and ask to give an extra sacrifice, because not a single Jewish soldier out of the twelve thousand was lost in the attack. That helps the reader imagine more clearly what this fighting must have been like—this was not two armies making war or even a hostile force raiding a city prepared in some small way for the assault. Instead, this was a massacre—thousands of men, women, and children killed, their town and homes destroyed, without a single death among the attackers, the Jewish warriors. And this is hardly the only moment in the Torah in which a clear and uncompromising violence toward enemies of the Jewish people is embraced—and even commanded.

The Moses we meet in Matot is especially troubling. This is not the Moses of liberation, leading the Jews from bondage; and this is not the Moses of exile, carried away by God as the Jews enter the Promised Land without him. This is the Moses of revenge. This is the Moses who commands armies, exercising power with what seems like a ruthless heart.

That we see this version of Moses specifically in connection to Midian is not accident. Just as the Jews near the end of their forty years of wandering through the desert as this part of the Bible unfolds, Moses himself wandered through the desert—and through Midian—after he first left Egypt alone and before returning to free the Jews from Pharaoh. Jethro, the sheikh who offered both his protection and his daughter to Moses, is a Midianite; and Mount Moriah, where Moses encountered God, seems to be located in Midian as well. Moses punishes the Midianites in part because some of the Midianite women seduced Jewish men, but he himself married a Midianite woman, Tzipporah. If his motive in Matot is to push back the temptations of the Midianites—idol worship and women among them—then we must recognize that he is fighting some elements of his own past and present as well.

■

Because every traditional congregation reads Matot every year and most rabbis who sermonize from the pulpit make at least some reference to the weekly Torah portion, commentaries on Matot abound. Some commentators avoid the slaughter of the Midianites entirely and discuss the other elements of the portion, including rules about honoring promises, and the role of the tribes of Gad and Reuven in the final assault on the people living in the land that will become Israel.

Some commentators suggest that Moses's acts should not be judged at all, because Moses is a figure above the judgment of ordinary men. Rabbi Joseph Telushkin, while acknowledging the brutality of Matot, points to the remark by Princeton philosopher Walter Kaufmann—translator of Nietzsche and author of the deeply rewarding *Critique of Religion and Philosophy*—that to accuse Moses of lacking moral conscience is almost impossible because so much of our notion of moral conscience comes, in fact, from our understanding of Moses himself. This is an interesting thought but hardly an argument. Could Moses possibly be exempt from the demands of virtue?

A third group acknowledges that the assault was harsh, but suggests that to protect Judaism as a faith, such extreme actions are justified, a variation on Michael Walzer's emergency ethics. Under the direst circumstances, *of course* a nation or a people will do almost anything to survive. In this case, the threat of the Midianites came in the form of their pagan religion, itself a debasement of Abraham's faith as a legacy of Abraham's son Midian, ancestor of the Midianites. To preserve the continuity of the Jews as Jews, wiping out the Midianites seems to a surprisingly broad range of commentators to be a reasonable moral compromise.

A fourth group of commentators hints at hidden meanings in the text. Are we perhaps intended to see Moses as clearly in the wrong, with this text teaching a subtle lesson through a drama of a good man acting badly? Both Rashi—the transformative eleventh-century commentator on the Torah—and the Lubavitcher rabbi Menachim Schneerson may be hinting at this in their comments on earlier lines in this Torah portion about making the kitchenware looted from the Midianite homes suitable for use by the Jews, an early source of some of the laws of keeping kosher. Rashi and Schneerson both note that Moses makes a small mistake in applying the rules of cleansing ritually unclean pots and pans. Moses errs, they suggest, because he was angry; and in Rashi's important words about the character of Moses, "anger produces error." But the close attention both giants of commentary offer on the koshering of dishes and vessels crowds out the commentary—commentary that never emerges—about the more glaring anger in Matot, leading to the massacre of a small city. In saying that anger produces error in koshering dishes and then failing to condemn the killing of men, women, and children a few lines later, the subtlety of the larger moral point becomes *so* subtle that no one is likely to see it at all.

A fifth group of commentators emphasizes the struggle to make sense of the violence in Matot. But even this group, with only the rarest exception, tends to turn away from the clear and literal meaning of the text. Rabbi Ismar Schorsch, head of the Conservative movement's Jewish Theological Seminary for many years, is one of the few influential rabbis to address the scale of the violence in Matot head on. He begins his commentary by talking about the mass killings by Jews directly, but then focuses on the theologically interesting question of one particular man killed, with no more concern for the other tens of thousands: "This week's *parashah* finds the Israelites routing the Midianites. The victory is total; the five kings of Midian and all their male subjects meet their death. The Torah appears to go out of its way to inform us that the Israelites 'also put Balaam son of Beor to the sword' (31:8)." Schorsch concludes his commentary by noting that

Jewish history attests the power of the spirit. . . .

. . . Even as we commemorate the destruction of two Temples and other dark moments of our history, we pay tribute to the unbroken faith and indomitable will of our people. Thus rabbinic Judaism rises from the ashes of the Second Temple, the talmudic academies of Ashkenaz after the First Crusade, Lurianic kabbalah after the Spanish expulsion and the State of Israel and the renaissance of American Judaism after the Holocaust. Mourning is the language of memory, the passage to recovery. As we move during the course of the day from lament to resolve, we affirm the primacy of the spirit in a world awash with violence.

Schorsch is thoughtful, subtle, and even inspiring in his concern for spirit—especially if one reads the commentary without looking at the biblical text. But with the Jewish slaughter of the Midianites in mind, affirming the primacy of spirit in a world awash with violence seems an extraordinary act of communal self-justification and a willful brushing aside of the core of the text.

Chapter 20 of Deuteronomy offers a counterpoint to Matot—at least at first glance. Reflective and humane, this part of the Torah instructs Jews in how to make war. It mandates that men who have recently been married or planted new fields or built new homes should not have to join in war and that when laying siege to a city, Jewish armies should first solicit a peaceful surrender, before attacking the inhabitants.

But these practices apply, it turns out, only "to all the cities that are very far from you." When fighting closer to home, against the tribes occupying land that God "gives you as an inheritance, you shall not allow any soul to live. Rather, you shall utterly destroy them." Why? "So that they should not teach you to act according to all their abominations that they have done for their gods, whereby you would sin against the Lord, your God" (Deut. 20:15, 16–17, 18).

In both cases—the story of the assault on the Midianites in Numbers and the command for all-out destruction of the specifically named local tribes in Deuteronomy—group identity is central to the violence. Those Midianite children in Matot are killed not because of anything they have done but because of who their parents are. Group identity is the very point and the precise object of Arendt's alternative view. When she offers Eichmann the prescription of reflective, individual thought, she is specifically offering an alternative to the ancient texts. Her ethic is an ethic of reflective individualism, directly rejecting the ethic of the tribe that we find throughout the Torah. Arendt—a Jewish scholar of Christian philosophy who was a modern writer and worldly citizen, whose chosen pulpit was the university lecture stand, and who never, as far as any of her friends or colleagues could recall, attended Jewish services—reflected the universalism that we find in Kant, Rousseau, and Jefferson, and not the tribalism of the Torah.

But this may be too simple a view. Michael Walzer delivered an engaging talk in 2001 to argue that a Jewish universalism is real and authentic; and while not found in the five books of Moses, it is at least close by in the biblical books of the Hebrew prophets. He begins his talk by acknowledging that the desire to find a Jewish universalism has a long history, driven by Jews who wrestled their more modern moral commitments backward into the Torah. "Throughout the enlightenment years, which in the case of the Jews extended from the last decades of the 18th century to the end of the 19th," he said, "prodigious efforts were made to discover a Jewish universalism or, better, to define Judaism as a universal religion of ethical reason." He continued:

But these were emancipated Jews, and even when the writers and activists among them looked to Jewish sources for their universalism—the creation of men and women in God's image, the liberation from Egyptian bondage, the prophetic critique of injustice, the vision of a general redemption—the actual creeds they espoused were more likely to derive from Kant or Marx than from the Bible or Talmud. Indeed, they could find what they needed in the Bible and Talmud to support a universalist politics and morality, but the discovery was too easy: they simply picked the nicest passages and ignored everything else.

And he is straightforward enough in his own initial statement of the facts: "Judaism is manifestly not a religion of ethical reason; no one looking at contemporary orthodoxy and ultraorthodoxy can have any illusions about that. Like the other world religions, it includes powerful rationalist and ethical doctrines—and Reform Jews especially have made the most of these; but it includes much else besides." The Torah, clearly, is a book in which Jews have special status, and other peoples are often explicitly rendered as less precious to God. But Walzer wants more from Judaism; and like the Marxists and Kantians he mentions in his opening, he finds it. Walzer looks beyond the texts and teachings of the early rabbis and toward the collective history of the Jewish people, where he finds traditions of tolerance and broadly humane ethics. And as discussed above, he also turns to the biblical Prophets, citing the passage from Amos that includes the line that has been translated to say, flatly, "To Me, O Israelites, you are just like the Ethiopians."

Walzer is certainly right that the debate over universalism has been an important part of Judaism at least since the era of the prophets, the very men who, as Martin Luther King noted in his "Letter from a Birmingham Jail," in "the eighth century B.C. left their villages and carried their 'thus saith the Lord' far beyond the boundaries of their home towns." It is not un-Jewish to say that we can and should wish Judaism to be centered more on humanity generally than on the tribe of Israel. The question is to what degree.

And for all the active debate about this question, the fundamental tribalism of Jewish identity has already been thoroughly overtaken by modern, reflective individualism in at least one important area, the cultivating of new generations of rabbis. A friend of mine illustrates the point. He occasionally joins a female Methodist minister to form the religious commentary team on a national morning television show. Millions of people tune in to hear this pair of good-looking spiritual leaders talk with the glossy program hosts about public issues with religious overtones, from abortion to terrorism to presidential elections. My friend graduated from the seminary of the Conservative movement and is as well qualified and credentialed as any traditional rabbi can be. But he's a boundary crosser, proudly bending the rules that hold back the spiritual heart of Judaism as he sees and feels it. And yet, on occasion, he volunteers that he is the eighth rabbi in his family line—a rabbi in every generation, from father to grandfather to great-grandfather and all the way back to the yeshivas of Europe two hundred years ago. He says this with a smile, and with a bit of irony, knowing that it offers the color of a good story.

He knows that his lineage makes him a more credible messenger of spiritual truth for many of his listeners. But he knows too that there is a side to his heritage that represents the narrowness of biblical Judaism. I think my friend understands that the Jews of the twenty-first century have chosen individual faith over covenant in determining who will become a rabbi and that his lineage is a symbol of the fixed laws of religious leadership that faded over the centuries, first into a tradition and then into a relic—a remnant of a kind of Judaism that the vast majority of Jews do not practice and cannot justify.

This could hardly be more different from the process of calling and discernment that Christianity has long embraced for the development of future ministers. "Many are called," the traditional Catholic teaching tells aspiring priests, "yet few are chosen." Would-be priests and ministers are expected to undergo extensive periods of study and self-reflection to understand whether they feel truly called to the church, without any regard to their lineage. And church leaders—following the tradition of discernment—examine those young men closely, often for years, to determine whether they are meant to be spiritual leaders of the church. Until recent decades, this would have stood as one of the starkest differences between the organizational dynamics of Christianity and Judaism, reflecting fundamental social and theological disagreements. Christianity emphasizes the individual's relationship with God. Judaism emphasizes the importance of human community as a moral center and moral source to a much greater degree. This points back to Walter Rauschenbusch's argument in *Christianity and the Social Crisis* that Christians need to be more like the Jewish prophets in their view of social justice. Rauschenbusch worried that American Christians were content with forgiveness from above for the sinful state of human life. Judaism insisted more clearly that sins against men and women must be made right in human terms before God could forgive the sinner. Yet the community that Judaism emphasizes—certainly in the five books of Moses—is a rigid one in which tribal lines are not crossed without punishment and the simple fact of parentage can mean life or death. To be a Jew might mean you deserve to live, while to be a Canaanite might mean you deserve to die. And to be a member of the Jewish lineage of the Kohanim would mean that you were destined for priestly duties and could not go to certain unholy places or do certain unholy things, whether you felt a calling or not. Feeling had little to do with one's role on Jewish communal and spiritual life. Identity was more the point.

And yet today the Reform, Conservative, and transdenominational seminaries have turned entirely away from the hereditary path; they recruit, they discern, and they ask applicants to examine their own souls, to discover and test their own paths toward spiritual leadership.

This is the text greeting prospective students, in 2010, on the web page for the Rabbinical School at Jewish Theological Seminary, the flagship of Conservative Judaism: "Our students are people of all ages and backgrounds who are seeking to integrate their passion for Judaism with a wide range of professional goals. Some students bring a love of music to their study of informal education or blend theater with Torah; some design special-education programs for day schools or plan environmental programs for camps. What do you want to do?"

Tradition, duty, and tribal lineage are absent in this statement. Instead, the call to serve and the will of the individual mark the entryway to this seminary. This is perhaps the most vivid example of the individualism of the modern age, of a personal sense of direct connection with truth and morality, prevailing over the traditional teachings of Judaism. It is an expression of Arendt's moral modernism prevailing over the biblical absolutes, an example of the argument being settled in practice, if not at all settled in theory. But if Jewish pluralists celebrate the victory of Enlightenment ethics, they must mourn the parallel decline in Jewish identity and worship. Hinging one's Jewishness on individual reflection and commitment has meant, by many measures, less Jewishness. If being Jewish has become a matter of choice, most Jews, most of the time, choose not to.

■

For Jews, loyalty is still a critical question: Shall we be more loyal to our religious identity than to our other identities? Is there any universal claim—as Kant would want there to be—on minimal standards of decency that we owe any other human, simply because of the very fact of humanity, without regard to Jewish identity? Another way to ask this question is to consider whether Judaism is a pathway to a higher sense of right and wrong, or a destination itself. Is there no higher good than the good of Jewishness? Or is Jewishness a way to live rightly, in line with some good that sits above the denominational goodness that speaks to Jews but not to others?

The biblical story of Amalek is the center of the Torah's answer to this question; Jewishness, it suggests, is the very essence of goodness and closeness to God. And some non-Jews should not be treated as fully human; some people, because of the actions of their ancestors, have no rights, no dignity, no claim to exist at all.

Amalek is about as bad as one can get in the bible. Descended from Esau—the unreflective man of unbridled appetites—Amalek led a band that cut off the weaker, trailing Jews in flight from Egypt and killed them. Because of this, God and Moses are without any reservation about killing all Amalekites—women, children, even their cattle. Deuteronomy 25 reads:

Remember what Amalek did unto thee by the way as ye came forth out of Egypt;

how he met thee by the way, and smote the hindmost of thee, all that were enfeebled in thy rear, when thou wast faint and weary; and he feared not God.

Therefore it shall be, when the LORD thy God hath given thee rest from all thine enemies round about, in the land which the LORD thy God giveth thee for an inheritance to possess it, that thou shalt blot out the remembrance of Amalek from under heaven; thou shalt not forget. (17–19)

A stark tribalism extends from this passage. Human decency does not extend to the Amalekites. When making war with these people, "thou shalt save alive nothing that breatheth" (Deut. 20:16).

Certainly among the Amelekites there must have been an Eichmann—an administrator, an order follower, a conformist who valued his group identity and did as he was told. He must die. His children, his wife, his grandchildren as well. There is no mercy for them. Their parentage determines their fate. Their claim to the full moral status of living men and women—as children of God—is a function not of what they do but of what their fathers and grandfathers have done. That is enough to warrant the ultimate punishment; and in the terms of the Hebrew Bible, it is just.

And yet there is more to Amalek than meets the eye. Deuteronomy presents Amalek as an external threat, a non-Jewish force that preys upon Jews, both literally—attacking the fleeing Jews trailing behind the main group departing Egypt as they begin to cross the Red Sea—and spiritually. In fact, Amalek is a common catchall for more-conservative Jewish theologians referring to the temptations of non-Jewish religious ideas and practices, the easy and indulgent spirituality of the material world. But the origins of Amalek go back to the story of Jacob and Esau, and actually lay the groundwork for Arendt's twentieth-century view of evil. Amalek is not an outside force at all, but a strand of the Jewish people, twisted away from the path of God.

Jacob and Esau were the twin sons of Isaac, bound in conflict beginning in the womb (God told Rebekah, their mother, "Two nations are in thy womb" [Gen. 25:23]). Jacob was reflective, gentle, his mother's favorite. Esau was bold, a hunter, favored by his father. At his mother's behest, Jacob fooled his father as he was dying and received the blessing intended for Esau. Esau, true to his nature, swore to kill Jacob as soon as Isaac died. Fearing for Jacob's life, Rebekah told him to flee to Padan-aram, the land of her brother Laban. Jacob lives there for twenty years. Laban famously fools Jacob into marrying his older daughter Leah, though Jacob loves his younger daughter Rachel. Only after a total of fourteen years of servitude to Laban does Jacob get to marry Rachel as well. (The story of Jacob, Laban, Leah, and Rachel echoes bits and pieces of the story of Jacob, Esau, and Isaac, with contests between the siblings, false blessings, an unhappy father, and divine prophecies guiding Jacob.)

Finally God sets Jacob on his way back home, along with his wives, their servants (two of his wives' handmaidens have borne Jacob's children as well), and hundreds of animals representing Jacob's accumulated wealth from his years working the land for Laban. Jacob's inevitable encounter with Esau draws closer. Jacob's servants report that Esau is on his way, along with four hundred men, to intercept Jacob and his caravan. Jacob sends off all the others and prepares to meet Esau alone. Night falls and he sleeps.

As with the story of the Tower of Babel, what happens next becomes one of the most written-about sections of the Torah, but it comes and goes in only a few lines:

And Jacob was left alone; and there wrestled a man with him until the breaking of the day.

And when he saw that he prevailed not against him, he touched the hollow of his thigh; and the hollow of Jacob's thigh was strained, as he wrestled with him.

And he said: "Let me go, for the day breaketh." And he said: "I will not let thee go, except thou bless me."

And he said unto him: "What is thy name?" And he said: "Jacob."

And he said: "Thy name shall be called no more Jacob, but Israel; for thou hast striven with God and with men, and hast prevailed."

And Jacob asked him, and said: "Tell me, I pray thee, thy name." And he said: "Wherefore is it that thou dost ask after my name?" And he blessed him there. (Gen. 32:24–29)

This encounter revisits the central events of Jacob's blessing by Isaac. Isaac, blind in his old age, heard Jacob's voice but felt the animal skin Jacob had draped over his arm to seem more like his hairy brother Esau. Isaac asked him, Who are you? Are you Jacob? Jacob lied, and Isaac gave him the blessing intended for Esau. Now, twenty years later, when asked his name, Jacob tells the truth and receives a blessing based, it seems, on his endurance through the night's struggle.

But whom is he encountering here? He asks flat out but does not receive an answer (he receives the blessing instead). The next line in the text is particularly important: "And Jacob called the name of the place Peniel: 'for I have seen God face to face, and my life is preserved.'" So Jacob feels sure he has seen God face to face—that he has become a prophet, though his prophecy is physical, the message of God written into his body. His night-wrestling partner seems to agree, bestowing on Jacob the name Israel—most commonly translated as "wrestles with God," though the translation of the noun built into that word-phrase, "el," can mean at its most literal "power" or "powers." Indeed, one of the common names for God in the five books of Moses, "Elohim," can raise a flicker of doubt about the Jewish claim to monotheism, because it takes the singular form of "el" and makes it plural. Our god, taken literally, may be a collection of powers rather than a bearded figure in the clouds.

Most Jews and Christians will know this story as the tale of Jacob Wrestling with the Angel, and several striking and important paintings depict the scene with precisely that title (those of Rembrandt and Dore are perhaps the best known). This is obviously different from wrestling with God, and the text seems intentionally ambiguous. The voice of the text itself says that Jacob "wrestled a man," though the Hebrew can arguably be rendered as "wrestled someone." Still, we might expect that if it really was God himself, that scene-setting line would make the point. The wrestler himself says that Jacob "hast striven with God," but that's vague enough to allow that Jacob has done this indirectly—perhaps to wrestle God's angel is to strive with God—or sometime in the past. And finally, we read that Jacob himself seems sure that he has now seen God face to face. Jacob's prophetic feeling might be his own misunderstanding of what has just happened—we get none of the clarity, for example, of God's presence at Mount Moriah. "And it came to pass," that earlier text from Genesis begins, ". . . that God did prove Abraham, and said unto him: 'Abraham'; and he said: 'Here am I.' And He said: 'Take now thy son, thine only son, whom thou lovest, even Isaac, and get thee into the land of Moriah.'" Even though an angel plays an intermediary role to stay Abraham's hand at the critical moment, the reader knows that the text means the entire event to be God's testing of Abraham. We know the role God plays, and we know the role the angel plays. We know who is who—and that, itself, is a key element of the story. It is Abraham, the first Jew, who gets the question of self-knowledge just right. He is the man who says Henaini, "I am here," and is fully present. Jacob similarly knows his own name and knows where he is. Indeed, he might know too much—knowing, it seems, that he has beheld God face to face, when the text plants the seeds of doubt for the reader.

Some rabbinic commentators—including Rashi—say that

Jacob specifically wrestled with the guardian angel of Esau, who can also be tracked back to the tempting angel who led Eve astray in the Garden of Eden. The text itself does not mention Esau, but a strong rabbinic tradition has emerged, beginning before Rashi and extending especially among Orthodox commentators today, to link Esau to the angel and to link that angel to a spirit of darkness woven through the bible, with some specifically saying that the angel in question is a version of Satan. It's important to note, though, that this is far more the work of the interpreters than it is of the text itself. Esau is certainly a sinful figure—lusty, impulsive, and full of appetites—but so again is Jacob, who is dishonest at the most crucial moment and who is at times too calculating to do the simple good he might do. Yet it is Esau who becomes the figure of real evil and indeed the progenitor of Amalek.

Where Jacob went to Laban's domain and married his daughters, keeping the circle of family and covenant whole, Esau married two local Hittite women, who made Rebekah and Isaac unhappy. Esau married outside the circle; and partly out of spite, he compounds his transgression by taking another wife, a daughter of Ishmael, son of Abraham and Hagar the servant. This presents the reader with a clear challenge of trying to understand not only who is a Jew but also the nature of evil. Ishmael is a son of Abraham but outside God's covenant, so he is, therefore, not a Jew. Esau, born into the covenant, is cheated out of his blessing by his brother and turns away from the covenantal path, in part by marrying women outside the circle of Judaism. His marriage to Ishmael's family only deepens the split in his identity and ultimately lays the foundation for an understanding of evils—like "Amalek," taken metaphorically—as being the self gone astray, rather than the Other that they often seem to be.

The Talmud—written in exile—outlines the three necessary steps to rebuild the temple in Jerusalem: first, Jews
must appoint a king; second, they must kill the descendants
of Amalek; and third, they may then rebuild the temple.
The foundational enumeration of 613 laws of Judaism by
twelfth-century scholar Maimonides includes three laws related to Amalek: to remember the bad deeds of Amalek, to
not forget what Amalek had done, and to "eradicate the seed
of Amalek."

Amalek is the grandson of Esau. After Esau married the
daughter of Ishmael, they had a son, Eliphaz, who in turn
was the father of Amalek, whose name seems to come from
his role as the chief of a region called Amalek (Gen. 36:16).
He is a direct and close descendant of Abraham, but he is the
product of marriages that led Jewish men further and further
from the covenant, and further from the Jewish family. The
Hebrew Bible turns back to Amalek again and again, and the
message is clear: remember what he did and destroy his children, his grandchildren, and all his descendants. Not only is
Amalek evil (clear from his actions); but all evil, it seems, is
Amalek. More than a metaphor, Amalek is the gesture of evil
as the losing of the way, the turning against family and God.

■

Early twentieth-century Jewish philosopher Martin Buber
offers a view of evil that harkens back to Jacob wrestling the
angel. Evil, for Buber, is a real presence, but not in the sense
of a dark angel or aberrant political force, like Nazism. Buber can agree with Arendt that we must guard against the evil
within ourselves, evil as an element of character and collective temptation; but he does not share the view of the Christian philosopher Augustine, for whom evil is essentially an
absence, cured by the presence of good. Instead, Buber sees

good and evil twined together, evil never entirely defeated and always offering cautionary lessons. In fact, for Buber the ongoing presence of evil can lead to a more-passionate and more–deeply committed engagement with the good.

Evil, in Buber's view, is not entirely opposed to good but instead is woven in the substance of spiritual life—a presence, a marking point, a source of passion. Scholar Maurice Friedman suggests that, for Buber, "good can be maximized not through the rejection or conquest of evil but only through the transformation of evil, the use of its energy and passion in the service of the good."

"The crucial religious experiences of man," Buber himself writes, "do not take place in a sphere in which creative energy operates without contradiction, but in a sphere in which evil and good, despair and hope, the power of destruction and the power of rebirth, dwell side by side. The divine force which man actually encounters in life does not hover above the demonic, but penetrates it." And so evil is not to be destroyed, as the masses surrounding the Eichmann trial suggested, or cured, as in Augustine's sense, but kept in mind as part of the human experience. There is a difference, Buber suggests, between the good that exists entirely on its own terms (a naive goodness) and the good that knows evil (a positive presence aware of its own boundaries and what stands beyond). This second kind of goodness has a greater meaning and impact on the world, because it is a goodness that implies struggle, spiritual and material.

Think; Decide

Still, Buber and Arendt share a fundamental vision. Evil, Buber says, "is lack of direction." He adds, "If there were a devil, it would not be one who decided against God, but who, in eternity, came to no decision." Where Arendt says, *think*, Buber says, *decide*. For both, though, it is the process—the process of thinking, the process of deciding—in which virtue sits, rather than merely in the ends, in the thoughts and decisions arrived at. Neither would take comfort in the destruction of Eichmann, because each is so deeply aware of evil as a part of ordinary human experience, not merely as an external force to be fought and destroyed.

Indeed, *Time* magazine reported on March 23, 1962, that

For two hours in Buber's house on Love of Zion Street [in Jerusalem], [Israeli premier David] Ben-Gurion listened while Buber pleaded with him to commute the Eichmann death sentence. Society is merely a group of persons, argued Buber, and when it kills one man, it is killing part of itself.

"Who gave society the right to kill itself?" he asked. "Society does not have such plenipotentiary rights." (Israel has no capital punishment except for high treason in wartime, war crimes against humanity or the Jewish people.)

In Eichmann's case, Buber added, execution would nurture another antichrist myth and permit a second-rate individual to symbolize the tragedy of European Jewry; his death would only offer easy, vicarious expiation to the guilty.

Eichmann *was* executed, with the wide support of the citizens of Israel.

Buber had lived in Israel since the mid-1930s and was generally seen as a Zionist though his view was, inevitably, not so simple. He wrote that "Zion means a destiny of mutual perfecting. It is not a calculation but a command; not an idea but a hidden figure waiting to be revealed. Israel would lose its own self if it replaced Palestine by another land and it would lose its own self if it replaced Zion by Palestine."

The Hebrew Bible takes for granted that Jews face the challenges of governing. The five books of Moses presume that being Jewish is, in part, a question of how to govern a community and its affairs, public and private, in addition to matters of divinity and worship. And in fact, these questions about governing *become* matters of divinity and worship, specifically because Judaism recognizes no separation between church and state. Writer Sidney Hyman—a secular Chicago-based writer about politics and culture for much of the twentieth century, whose father was an influential Orthodox rabbi in Gary, Indiana—talked often about what he saw as the difference between the Hebrew and Christian Bibles. The Hebrew Bible was written by people who were already governing, Hyman emphasized, and so it is filled with the weighty questions of administration, how much to charge in taxes, how to resolve disputes, where the limits of freedom needed to be drawn for the sake of the common good. In contrast, the early Christians had no state to run, and so they could promise anything.

The creation of the State of Israel gave the Jews of the world something extraordinary—and it took something away as well. Hyman's glib but penetrating comment gets to the heart of it. With a state, the burdens of governing, of protecting borders, of enforcing the law bring the religious spirit down to the darkest corners of society. With a state, the dark compromises of material society—of getting and spending, giving and taking—become the substance of a religion's daily exchange with its followers (and with others). Without a state, religious vision is not challenged—not diluted—by the practical compromises of governing, the application of divinity to the smallest tasks and imperfect systems of daily life. Buber insisted that the state must err on the side of divinity and refrain from the acts that might be useful but ultimately would demean the religious character not only of the state but of the Jewish people. Ben-Gurion—along with Hausner, the prosecutor; the panel of judges facing Eichmann; and the large majority of the Israeli people—felt differently.

Which side of this argument offers the Jewish future we seek? There has not been another Eichmann and there has not been another Holocaust in the decades since the trial. Yet there have been ten thousand smaller acts to challenge the State of Israel, the Jewish people, and humanity. When Israeli reservists joke that they have become agents of the Gestapo, we see a future that we should not tolerate.

Strength or virtue? How much of each, in what measure? Golda Meier offers an insightful answer to this question in her comment to Sadat ("We can forgive you for killing our sons. We cannot forgive you for forcing us to kill yours"): enough strength to ensure that the Jewish people are not overrun or overwhelmed in the lands on which they live but enough virtue to withhold forgiveness for our own worst acts and worst natures.

First survive, but answer the question, *as what?* We are charged by our sacred texts to be a people that seeks always to do and to be better, a people with a sacred duty to help heal all the souls in the world. When we put down these tasks for the sake of survival, even for a moment, we must know how awful a bargain it is that we strike. We must constantly remind ourselves of our own failures to be fully Jewish for the sake of survival.

■

A Conservative rabbi in the United States recently shared with me his commitment to this position in surprising terms —coming more from a left, social-justice perspective. Rather than make the more common argument among Orthodox

Zionists that Jews should govern as Jews because God gave the land to them, he argues that Jews have the special obligation to govern because that is the best way to serve the mission of tikkun olam.

The mission of being Jewish, of embracing a special duty to live Jewishly specifically to heal the world, requires that we have a Jewish state, governed with Jewish aims. It has to be a better place, truer to the vision of a good world created by a just God than other states. To separate the religious vision from the state is not a Jewish view—it cuts off a central theme of the Torah and turns away from so much of the rabbinical tradition. You can see, from the debates we face, how much we lose in the short term and how the argument can so easily turn against us, because we hold onto this part of the covenant of being Jewish, but this is the role we are here to play. To pretend otherwise is to reject so much of the Torah and thousands of years of teachings.

To be sure, most of the official doctrine of the principal Jewish religious movements—Reform, Conservative, and Reconstructionist—take an opposing view and support the separation of church and state to large degrees. The Orthodox communities, in contrast, generally take a hard line, based on biblical texts.

And without a doubt, the harshest biblical view of the Jewish state is still present among a meaningful number of Jewish people. Commentator Laura S. Zarembski described, in 2000, the demographic slice of the Israeli population that gives "allegiance to the State of Israel on the basis of religious beliefs. They perceive the modern Jewish state as a reflection of the continuing covenant between God and the Jewish people and recognize the authority currently governing Israel in that light. They make up two thirds of the religious community and approximately eight percent of the total population," or about 650,000 people, and have a meaningful number of allies outside of Israel.

Hannah Arendt's position, in contrast, is not so much partisan as cautionary. If we govern, she suggests, we must guard against the pull of authoritarianism, of loyalty to the state and its bureaucracy, because the highest kind of moral expression happens above the level of the state—any state, including a Jewish state.

■

The photo of Eichmann's trial offers a specific challenge for the future of Judaism: Can we build our civic and social institutions with maximum strength and cohesion, while also strengthening individual, reflective thought? Can we build strong institutions—and perhaps even nations—while encouraging the heterodox, the radical challenges, and the kind of original views of the world that stand against what Eichmann was and represented?

Avigdor Lieberman, for one, says no. In 2006, while he was deputy prime minister of Israel, Lieberman offered comments that seem almost tailored to oppose Arendt's arguments against thoughtless loyalty, as reported in the *New York Sun*:

Mr. Lieberman spoke of requiring Israelis to sign a commitment to loyalty to the Israeli flag and to its national anthem, and of requiring service in the army or alternative national service. Citizens who refuse to sign the declaration, he said, could continue as permanent residents of Israel, working, studying, and receiving health care benefits, but they could not vote in national elections or be elected to national office.

"It's not racism," Mr. Lieberman said. "The test is loyalty, not their religion." He said he would also deny Israeli citizenship to extreme anti-Zionist Orthodox Jewish groups, such as the Neturei Karta, which sent representatives to this week's Holocaust denial conference in Tehran.

Mr. Lieberman said the "close linkage" between Israeli Arabs and the Arabs of the Palestinian Authority is a result of Israeli "weakness."

"If we will be more strong, more tough, they will be more loyal," he said.

In contrast, former speaker of the parliament in Israel, Avraham Burg, wrote in a recent and controversial book about Israel's future that "if we do not establish modern Israeli identity on foundations of optimism, faith in humans and full trust in the family of nations, we have no chance of existing." Burg believes that the demands of loyalty to Israel and of loyalty to the Jewish people have pushed Israel to the point of destruction—destruction of its soul as a truly democratic nation and potentially destruction in the most literal sense. Only an absolute democratic commitment, rooted in the kind of universalism Michael Walzer acknowledged to be largely missing from the core Jewish scriptures, will save Israel according to Burg. The current model of Jewish-democratic Israel, he says, has no future. "It can't work anymore," Burg told Israeli daily newspaper *Ha'Aretz*. "To define the State of Israel as a Jewish state is the key to its end."

■

Hannah Arendt's close friend and teacher, the German philosopher Karl Jaspers, wrote her, as she began planning her trip to Israel to cover the Eichmann trial, that "something other than law is at issue here—and to address it in legal terms is a mistake. . . . Israel is not the Jewish people. . . . The

Jewish people are more than the state of Israel, not identical with it. If Israel were lost, the Jewish people would still not be lost."

In October 1964—after the trial, after *Eichmann in Jerusalem* and the first wave of response and resistance to it—Arendt sat for a television interview in West Germany. During the interview, she said:

the Jewish religion is a national religion. The worldlessness which the Jewish people suffered in being dispersed, and which—as with all people who are pariahs—generated a special warmth among those who belonged, changed when the state of Israel was founded. . . . [O]ne pays dearly for freedom. The specifically Jewish humanity signified by their worldlessness was something very beautiful. . . . Of course, a great deal was lost with the passing of all that. One pays for liberation. . . . I know that one has to pay a price for freedom. But I cannot say that I like to pay it.

That price, it seems, is part of Sidney Hyman's notion of the Hebrew Bible's special role as the book of a people that governs. The necessary facts of governance rob the people of the innocence that powerlessness can bestow. This is not necessarily a religious question, but it is a question for any religion that makes claims to govern, as Judaism does (and Islam as well, though Christianity much less so). This is the same question that the photo of Eichmann before the bar offers us: how much to weight survival and strength and how much to weight virtue and reflection.

Arendt makes the best argument for virtue that one can imagine, and it is convincing. But she clearly sees it as the argument that must nip at the edges of the practical and perhaps even brutal commitment to survival at the core of any state.

■

If there is to be a future of the Jewish people, it will come because of a Jewish toughness that sits in dialogue with Jewish virtue, with Jewish tribalism in dialogue with a modern Jewish ethic of individual faith and virtue. Martin Buber paints the picture: the darkness of survival's brutality has never been entirely removed or rejected but has been woven through the cloak of virtue and reflective, thoughtful statecraft that we prefer to wear.

As Arendt suggests, if the Jewish people are to survive, we will pay the price for freedom. And like Arendt, we will not like paying it.

The oldest written Torah document that has been conclu-
sively dated was comitted to scrolls of parchment in the
seventh century BCE. The seventh-century scrolls were only
found in 1979 when archaeologist Gabriel Barkay began
digging in an area of the Old City of Jerusalem known as
the Valley of Hell. Barkay told the *New York Times* that
"after 120 years of great archeologists digging in Jerusalem, you don't expect to find very much. We were totally
unprepared for what we discovered." The text contained a
blessing from Numbers. "Finding this text is something very
moving for me," Professor Barkay said. "It is the text my
father used to bless me with when I was a boy. It is found
today in every Jewish prayer book. I was not digging for
my roots. I was on a scientific dig looking for the truth in a
particular site. But you cannot help but be touched by the
thought of people uttering the same verses in the same city
for 2,600 years."

CHAPTER SIX

The Fifth Photograph

One of the bittersweet contradictions of Jewish worship typically occurs twice in most Jewish services, when the rabbi (but not always the rabbi, sometimes an honored member of the congregation or a bar mitzvah boy) leads a procession around the pews and down the central aisle, holding the Torah. The scrolls are generally dressed in fine velvet coverings, with silver breastplates hanging from the scroll handles and each capped by a silver crown. The breastplate and crowns are generally ornate and sometimes stunning. As the procession passes, congregants lean over each other to reach toward the scrolls, touching a prayer book or the corner of a prayer shawl to the velvet, and then kiss the book or cloth. The Torah is revered.

And yet this seems exactly the opposite of the foundational teaching of the Torah itself, that Jews shall not worship anybody or anything other than God himself. If an outsider knowing nothing about Jewish religion attended a typical Jewish service, the scrolls—kept in an elevated chamber before the whole congregation, unveiled with great ceremony and honor, draped in velvet, adorned with breastplate and crowns—would surely seem to be an idol, a small god kept and worshipped. And just as surely, rabbis and other Jewish leaders have heard this criticism before. Some agree and push their congregations to a more modest regard for the scrolls as objects, while continuing to rever their content. But most dismiss the criticism. The Torah is God's gift to the Jewish people, they say, and our love of the Torah is a love of our connection to God. It is not worship but celebration.

Noted Conservative rabbi Arthur Herzberg struck an appealing balance in a story he told about a man he'd met in Germany, a Catholic priest. "He wanted me to think well of him, so he told how as a parish priest in 1943 in a city under Nazi occupation, he had hidden a scroll of the Torah, which a Jew had brought to his rectory. I could not stop myself from asking him: 'Why did you not hand the Nazis the Torah and hide the Jew?'" Hertzberg's story is meant to have a lesson beyond his chastisement of the priest in absentia: he's telling us that the choice is awful but not difficult. Save the man; sacrifice the scrolls. The greatest scrolls are not remotely as precious as the worst man.

"The love for the Torah," one Jewish woman told me recently, "is an enormous love. It's a love of being Jewish, a love of the generations who came before us, a love of the vision and the dream of God's love of man. The Torah is the proof we can hold in our hands that this is more than a vision and more than a dream. The Torah represents the reality of God's love for the Jewish people—that the dream is true."

But another woman, studying to be a rabbi at a transdenominational seminary, sees a warning as well as a dream in the physical presence of the scrolls:

I wonder how we can make the choice between the scrolls as a sacred object, and the scrolls as a starting point for a tradition that questions and challenges the received wisdom. I love the Torah for two reasons. I love it because of the tradition it represents, because of the continuity over the centuries, knowing that the Torah was there a thousand years ago, and a hundred years ago, and that it's still here. And I love it because of the story of creation, and the story of freedom, and the questions and conversations and challenges that come with it. But if we take it as an object and make it holy, we start to move the power of Judaism away from the experience of the people and too much into a box. The box can be a scroll or a temple or an eruv, but it's all about boundaries and limits and who owns the scrolls or the building or even who gives the blessing you think you need to be good or pure or holy. The greatest revelation of worship is that no one owns it. No book, no box, no place is the key—*you* are the key.

Jamie Korngold, a Reform rabbi living in Colorado, sees the Torah in similar terms. She is particularly troubled by Dueteronomy, the book that focuses most on ritual practice. "In 622 BCE," she writes, "the priests of the Temple made an incredible discovery. They found a fifth book of the bible, and it contained just the passage they needed." Needed, she argues, to shift the power of Judaism from the mountaintop and open-sky worship of Genesis and Exodus to the duly measured-out and sanctified holy places controlled by the priests. "Do not worship the Lord as the non-Jews do," Deuteronomy commands, "but look only to the site that the Lord will choose amid all your tribes as his habitation to establish His name there" (12:4–5). That's the passage that Korngold sees as the preists' self-justifying discovery—or invention. It seems to be saying, Look to the temples, look only to the places that the priests control, to find God.

"With this monumental discovery" of the text of Deuteronomy, Korngold writes, "the people stopped worshipping on the high places, and the Temple became the center of Jewish practice, a tradition which has been passed on to the synagogues and churches of today."

Structured as a trio of sermons by Moses, Deuteronomy is especially conscious of the temptations of pagan worship and seems to clamp down on the freer spirit of worship in the earlier books, at least in part because the priests felt pressure from competing religions. The spirit of a community encountering its God and composing an initial, shared understanding of that God has faded. The encounter with the devine in Deuteronomy seems more about the borders and edges of Judaism than about the center and spirit of it.

On the one hand, this glimpse of the internal tension within the Torah makes it easier for some to revere the scrolls, because they contain a teaching built of dialogue, negotiation, and reconsideration. Add this fifth and final book to the earlier four, and rather than finding a fixed, unchanging text, we find a shifting field of ideas, a world in motion animated by a profound commitment to the God whose name is "I will become." On the other hand, there is an important job for the Torah as the pillar of faith, as a guidepost that ought to serve as a strong and stationary support. It helps if the Torah can mean something specific and eternal, so that we can lean on it when we need to. This need for clarity moves us to ask, which vision is the right one? And because Deuteronomy is the last of the five books, it seems to own the last word. But this claim to the last word is not limited to Deutronomy at all. With every new layer of scripture and rabbinic interpretation, the urge to declare the game over seems to come along as well. The question of which last word we accept on its own terms is very much up to us.

■

The poet Robert Frost famously said that writing free verse, poetry without rhyme or formal structure, is like playing tennis without a net. Finding the right degree of tension in the

Torah is similar. If we allow the text to take on any meaning we prefer, we can all be Torah-centered Jews, but that center won't mean much. And yet if we take the opposite position and insist on strict literalism, our active participation in the making of meaning is lost. At one extreme, any religion becomes rule-bound and rote. At the other, it becomes whatever its followers wish it to be and inevitably loses its claims to be whole and distinct.

Rule-bound religion leads to acts that are harsh and cold in spirit, excused by the black-letter texts of scripture, while the ultimate expression of its opposite is faith as a fleeting choice ("Today I am a Jew; tomorrow, a Buddhist; Thursday, I will be a Christian; and the next day, all three"). To make religion complete—to make it rhyme, in Frost's sense—we need to find the point of balance where the competing approaches (leading the Torah, or being led by it) can coexist in the right measure, to create a viable and meaningful whole.

This challenge finds its way into my own house when my son, eleven, tells me that he does not believe in Judaism. It's a timely comment. Our synagogue has asked us to fill out any number of forms (and get up-to-date on our dues and contributions) so they can assign us a bar mitzvah date two years hence. It's an eight hundred–family community, with hundreds of children. We will be lucky if they assign us a date remotely close to our son's thirteenth birthday, and there's a good chance we'll share the occasion with another family, double bar mitzvahs edging toward the rule rather than the exception. So it's helpful to learn that, for the moment, he does not want a bar mitzvah at all.

My son considers himself spiritual. He's thinking maybe of a vision quest in the American Indian tradition instead of a bar mitzvah, and he's been doing some research. He now tells us that a vision quest turns out to be less of a life-or-death solo wilderness trek than he'd first thought. It seems more likely to involve drawing a circle in the woods with a ten-foot diameter and then sitting in the middle for three or four days without food, waiting for a vision.

A vision quest has some appeal to me, I tell him. Could it perhaps be part of an enhanced bar mitzvah? Could he do both? He thinks not, but he was impressed by the notion that Moses going up Mount Saini and encountering the burning bush was a vision quest of a certain kind.

To keep the conversation with my son going, I borrow a wonderful teaching tool from Rabbi Irwin Kula. Irwin likes to draw out people who say "I don't believe in God," by asking about the characteristics of the God they don't believe in. Then he draws a box, puts all of those qualities in the box, and generally is able to say with a clear conscience, "You know what? I don't believe in this God either. But let me tell you about the God I do believe in." So I try to get my son to explain what this Judaism he rejects is like. He has some useful answers. It's about a God who looks like a rabbi and tells people what to do. It does not have much passion in it. It comes to you from books, often in Hebrew and hard to read even when they're in English.

For contrast, we take a moment and read, together, a bit of Ralph Waldo Emerson's 1837 book *Nature*. It starts this way: "The foregoing generations beheld God and nature face to face; we, through their eyes." My son gets this right away. He'd like to hear more. Emerson goes on to ask,

Why should not we also enjoy an original relation to the universe? Why should not we have a poetry and philosophy of insight and not of tradition, and a religion by revelation to us, and not the history of theirs? . . . Why should we grope among the dry bones of the past, or put the living generation into masquerade out of its faded wardrobe? The sun shines to-day also. There is more wool and flax in the fields. There are new lands, new men, new thoughts. Let us demand our own works and laws and worship.

My son decides that he loves Ralph Waldo Emerson. We begin to talk about Emerson's idea of God. In time, we talk about some Jewish alternatives to the God who looks like a rabbi and lives in old books. I'm still hoping that we can do the vision quest *and* the bar mitzvah and that our son can use his own struggle for meaning as a teaching tool as he addresses and leads a congregation—this is what a good bar mitzvah is all about. I hope I'm not selling Judaism too hard, though. My son thinks I am. I'm trying to use a gentler touch.

I'm not sure my son's current trajectory will lead him to Judaism as I understand it. I'm afraid that the heart of Judaism is in some ways opposed to the visionary connection with God that Emerson talks about. Heschel captures this when he says that in Judaism, man never stands before God alone; the Torah and Israel are always beside him. I find this powerful, challenging, and attractive. My son certainly would not, at least not yet. What he wants, quite specifically, is to stand before God alone. Heschel's spiritual view is humane and generous, but he does insist on reading the Torah with respect for what it is and what it is not. He is not a rabbi prepared to let the individual make of the Torah only what he or she wants it to be. Not since Moses has the role of the Jew been to stand alone, and Heschel would not want my son to feel that he can reshape Judaism to fit his own spiritual journey.

Indeed, one of the closing lines of Dueteronomy is clearly the text that Emerson writes against in *Nature*: "And there hath not arisen a prophet since in Israel like unto Moses," the text of the English Revised Version translation reads, "whom the Lord knew face to face" (34:10). Yet it is precisely that face-to-face connection that Emerson wants—demands, even—and that I remember as a revelation when I read it for the first time as a graduate student, studying Emerson without ever having read Deuteronomy.

Still, I have a feeling that my son's passionate desire for a direct and original connection to God and the universe is not an end but a point along a path, one that can lead back to community. I hope that with a glimpse of divnity in his heart, my son can find his way to seeing that same divinity in the people beside him. I hope he'll see that standing before God with Torah and Israel at your side can mean that God himself is alongside, and within, and not exclusively above in that sense that my son, perhaps rightly, resists.

In wanting his own face-to-face connection to God, my son is not specifically rejecting Torah or Israel. In fact, like most of us, he knows too little about the Torah to reject it. What he's doing is more like ignoring it. But as he learns more—and the lessons can take decades, even lifetimes—I expect he'll see that the Jewish engagement with Torah is itself a kind of vision quest, an encounter with the heart of Judaism. Unfortunately, some of his current teachers give him the impression that this heart of Judaism can be sliced up into lessons, rules, and diagrams and served to students in an orderly sequence without any particular danger to the soul of the young Jew. Torah is certainly not that.

The Torah—literally, "the teaching"—can mean a number of things. Most formally, it refers to the scrolls containing the five books of Moses, also known as the *Chumash*. The larger collecton of Jewish scripture, containing the books of the Prophets and the Writings (the Khetuvim, "writings," includes the Psalms, the book of Job, and eleven other fundamental texts) as well as the five books of Moses, is called the *Tenakh*—an acronym of *T* for Torah, *N* for Nevi'im ("prophets"), and *Kh* for Khetuvim. Some call this collection the Jewish Bible. Some call the whole thing the Torah—though more often, the reference would be to "torah" rather than "the Torah," referring to the teachings rather than to the scrolls.

The five books of Moses are divided by tradition into fifty-four weekly sections, or *parshot*, each of which is read—and often discussed—in worship services as the year unfolds. The synagogues in Buenas Aires, in Brooklyn, and in Bombay will read the same passage at the same time (though in Israel the schedule of Torah portions is often off by one day from the Diaspora calendar).

This centrality of the five books of Moses establishes something of a hierarchy—the five books are the Torah on the scrolls that we hold before us when we worship, the stories that we retell and study every year. The Prophets and the Writings are vitally important as well and form much of the basis for the daily prayers in most synagogues, but they are not retold in the same way and not represented by worship objects (like the scrolls) that stand before the congregation in a holy tabernacle at the center of the synagogue.

■

The text of that concluding line in the last section of Deuteronomy that Emerson drew on is sometimes translated more forcefully than the version above. The King James Bible translates the line this way: "And there arose not a prophet since in Israel like unto Moses, whom the Lord knew face to face." But it is the Jewish Publication Society translation published in 1985 that begins with an especially resonant pair of words: "Never again did there arise in Israel a prophet like Moses—whom the Lord singled out, face to face."

"Never again," and yet the books of the Prophets—Amos and Joshua and Jeremiah among them—were yet to come. The adding-to nature of Jewish tradition, with the five books of Moses and then the Prophets and then the Writings and then the Talmud and then more, is quite hopeful for the young man or woman yearning to feel the presence of God directly, face-to-face. For better or worse, we have the sense that "Never again" might not really mean never again. That final book of the Torah makes a claim for completeness hard to square with the layering on of new texts generation by generation. Because Deuteronomy is viewed by many scholars as having been written two or three centuries after the first four books were completed, perhaps it betrays an anxiety that just as it adds on to and reshapes what came before, in time yet newer claims will arise to reshape the established meaning of the seemingly complete body of scripture. These final lines can feel like an attempt to say, "No more changes, no more dramatic interpretations. It's done."

How Done Is It? Finding the Middle Path

It's done. And yet how done is it? We know what comes next—the books of the Prophets. And then the Writings. And then the commentaries that form the kernel of the Talmud, and certainly this cycle is still unfolding. Some of the wisdom writings of our own age will be read in ages hence, and the whole of Jewish holy writings will be larger then than it is today. But all these new books and interpretations of the Jewish scriptures begin in the old, and each represents its own kind of middle path.

The idea of tikkun olam is a good example. The phrase "tikkun olam" first appeared in the earliest versions of the Aleynu prayer, originally part of the Rosh Hashanah annual service and now the most common concluding prayer in Jewish services year round. Only in the Mishna, the collection of rabbinic debates and judgments collected around the year 200 CE, was it first given more than fleeting attention, but even then it had a narrow purpose: to ensure that disadvantaged groups like slaves or divorced women were included under the protections of Jewish law. But the idea has grown over time in the rabbinic and mystic literature to encompass a special role for Jews as stewards of social justice, and it now suggests that the Jewish people have a divinely ordained role as a source of healing for the world. There's little doubt that as generations of Jews saw new challenges in the societies they inhabited and felt new strength to act for the broader social good, they began responding more fully to the bits and pieces of ancient Jewish texts that support social engagement and activism beyond what the rabbis of the Mishna were talking about. The Mishna opened a door that later generations walked through to build something original, but certainly in the spirit of the text and certainly within a framework that begins with the Torah. This is not a matter of tradition or scripture having either a vote or a veto. Rather, it is the spirit and the letter of tradition and text echoing in different proportion generation by generation.

And just as the Jews are imagined to play a special role to heal the world, so too the Torah is, potentially, a source of healing *for* the Jews. When there is a gap between what we feel and what we find in the Torah, we have the opportunity to step toward the Torah to close that gap, and we have the opportunity to pull the Torah toward us, though the most important spiritual work happens when these two alternatives are in fact joined together. We make a greater and truer whole when we reach toward the Torah in search of healing. We heal both ourselves and the vision of divinity that is broken when we stand apart from it. And that is much of what I see when I look closely at the photograph above.

This image of a woman repairing a Torah is striking for a number of reasons. Most of the scholars and artisans with the knowledge and commitment to repair Torah scrolls are very traditional—conservative with a small *c*—in their views of religious law. Allowing a woman to do this work is troubling to their worldview. And seeing the Torah itself as an object—a thing made up of constituent parts, the parchment clinging too loosely to its wooden spool as any scroll might, a rip in need of being sewn shut—is troubling in its own right. The idea of being deep inside the Torah not to receive a connection to God but instead to poke around, to repair and refigure what is there, gets at the most important debate about how Judaism ought to be felt and practiced.

Her eyes are sharply focused, and her hands are thin—delicate but strong. Another woman stands out of the frame of the photo and holds the scroll steady for her; only her hands are visible. It is a moment of great concentration. The photograph itself falls into two halves, divided by a line that begins at the bottom of the photo with a bit of tape or a patch on the rolled portion of the scroll and that carries directly upward, across the rabbi's face with a streak of light and up through the vertical line at the center of her yarmulka and through to the top of the photo, separating a corkboard from other objects. One side is open to the light, more plain, brighter; the other busier, darker, more rooted. Where her hands meet, repairing the Torah, the two halves of the photo meet, almost a hint at the general inclinations of heaven and earth touching as the scroll is stitched together.

The rabbi's hair is a bit wild, and gray streaks out from her forehead—anyone who remembers *The Ten Command-*

ments will remember Charleton Heston's Moses going up Mount Moriah to receive the tablets as a youngish man with contained, dark hair and coming back down looking like an ancient sage, wild hair streaked white and gray to match the faraway look in his prophet's eyes. But the rabbi in this photo is not looking up and away in awe. Instead she looks down and works. She is not a prophet focused on the horizon but the scholar who prays with the precise acts of her hands. Her head and shoulders are framed by a simple bookcase behind her. We don't see the window, but we do see a corner of its frame. And the daylight is clear, falling on the Torah, which sits unfurled sideways to the scribe, but straight on to the light in the window.

The prayer traditionally said before beginning Torah study opens this way: "Blessed are you Adonai, our God, king of the universe, who sanctified us with your commandments and commanded us to immerse ourselves in the Torah." But that phrase, "immerse ourselves," comes from one of the harder Hebrew words to translate—*la'asok*, which has its root in the word "to be busy." So the prayer tells us that God has commanded Jews to be busy with Torah, in the sense of working at it. We work at the Torah not simply to memorize it but to create a personal meaning of something divine, something beyond us, that we can make comprehensible. We work to bring the Torah within our reach, interpreting in ways that shape its meaning, that add the human to the divine, but also that necessarily narrow the full force and meaning of the Torah, because how else can we encounter divinity? We are not remotely able to comprehend it fully. Interpretation of Torah by definition will fall short.

The act of interpretaiton humbles the Torah, because it depends on our human abilities to see things that are greater than human. Interpretation also humbles us, measuring the human by a standard infinitely larger than human experience and understanding. Again, there is a middle path to be found: we must interpret the Torah to make it meaningful in our lives, but this is not to make the hand and mind of man replacements for those of God.

We immerse ourselves in the Torah not only so that we can be molded by it but also so that we can add our labor to it and leave our imprint on it, or at least on its presence in our lives. God's commandments are in the Torah, but here they fold back on themselves: we are commanded to get busy with the commandments, to examine them from every side, in every context, and to pull out all that might be built into them. In Psalm 119, this divergance is even more clear. "Bestow kindness upon Your servant," the Psalmist says to God. "I shall live and I shall keep Your word. Uncover my eyes and I shall look at hidden things from Your Torah." The meaning and importance of the Torah are not simple; they are not obvious. Or perhaps it is better to say that what is obvious about them is only a beginning. The hidden things take—and reward—work, interpretation, immersion.

■

The rabbi repairing the Torah in the photo above is named Linda Motzkin. She coleads a Reform synagogue with her husband in upstate New York. An article about her work as a scribe that appeared in the *Forward* explains the challenges and compromises that Motzkin faces in her work, particularly because the usual sellers of supplies to scribes do not want to sell to women:

Motzkin makes her own parchment out of deerskin, bounty given to her by local hunters, fashions quills from reeds or bird feathers, and ritually immerses herself in a neighbor's pond. The ink she uses was a gift from her teacher, but she is working with a congregant to brew her own. So far, they haven't made a batch to her liking, but she's still trying.

"Getting materials that are born out of an act of deception seems in contradiction to the very notion of writing a sacred text," Motzkin said. "Everything I'm doing is up-front. All the materials, everybody who's helped me make stuff are people who know what I'm up to and want to support it."

That respect for Halacha is part of Motzkin's process from the very beginning. After receiving a deerskin from the hunters, she recites a blessing as she begins to prepare the hides herself—soaking them in limewater, stretching them on wooden frames she has built, then sanding and trimming them to the proper texture and proportions.

Rabbi Motzkin rejects the idea that only men can be scribes but embraces the ritual demands of koshering her parchments, inks, and tools. It is "the very notion of writing a sacred text," she says, that guides her judgment of which rules matter. The word "writing" has a special meaning here—not creating the words but copying them, writing them physically. As Heschel talked of marching as a kind of prayer, Motzkin recognizes writing the sacred text as a kind of prayer as well. Heschel prayed with his legs, he said; and Motzkin prays with her hands. Both view making change as a prayerful act—going back to the Torah to work at it and to find new meaning within it. She is not trying to remake the Torah or to revise it or to reshape it to fit her personal choices. She is not stepping away from the Torah but toward it. She is working it, wrestling with it, which means much more than simply saying yes to every rule, restriction, and command.

But she does say no to a part of Torah, the part that excludes women from leadership as rabbis and scribes. To this extent, we have to recognize a step away from Torah. The challenge is to step away from the elements of Torah we cannot abide—stoning a disobedient child, for example—while finding some way to keep the Torah whole and preserve its integrity. In this sense, rather than the task of meeting God in the Torah being incomplete, it is too complete. All of divinity is in there, and more—and the more is part of the puzzle of Jewish commitment. Can we encounter, behold, and be connected to all that is there, while acting only on the parts that are meaningful and virtuous for our lives?

■

Consider the example of that disobedient child. While Mordechai Kaplan's answer to the challenge of making sense of the parts of Torah that we simply do not accept in our lives—that "the past has a vote but not a veto"—can seem glib, it holds a kind of integrity that more Torah-centered approaches actually lack. If the Torah says that a child who has disobeyed once too often is to be stoned to death and we are certain that this is wrong, Kaplan and broad segments of the Reform and Conservatve communities will have the courage to say that in this instance the Torah is wrong. Perhaps in a different age, in a different place, there was a decency to this teaching; but for us, for now, we respectfully say no.

However, the Talmudic discussion of this bit of Deuteronomy, chapter 21, part of Parshat Kit Tetze, reveals a different approach.

Here is the biblical text from the Jewish Publication Society's 1917 translation:

If a man have a stubborn and rebellious son, that will not hearken to the voice of his father, or the voice of his mother, and though they chasten him, will not hearken unto them;

then shall his father and his mother lay hold on him, and bring him out unto the elders of his city, and unto the gate of his place;

and they shall say unto the elders of his city: "This our son is stubborn and rebellious, he doth not hearken to our voice; he is a glutton, and a drunkard."

And all the men of his city shall stone him with stones, that he die; so shalt thou put away the evil from the midst of thee; and all Israel shall hear, and fear. (Deut. 21:18–21)

The discussion in the Talmud dwells in the details of language. The biblical text talks about a rebellious son, but its specific words suggest that he is old enough to be responsible for his own actions yet young enough still to be a boy. Therefore, the rabbis say, it only applies to boys of a very certain age. Among the other requirements before stoning their son, the parents must go before a group of religious judges and tell their story "in the same voice." This seems clearly to mean "in total agreement," but some commentators use this to suggest that the husband's voice must come from the mother's mouth. Because this is impossible, the criteria for the punishment can never be met—we can say that we'll follow the commandment yet define the commandment to be so narrow that it never applies. And so we get to feel that we obey the Torah without having to do what it says we must do. We give ourselves leave to find the Torah perfect, while in practical fact we reject what it clearly says.

Close reading is often deeply revealing, but this degree of analysis robs the text of any coherent meaning. It is a skillful way to adhere to the community value of living a life that follows the Torah while in fact, with a wink and a nod, forcing the Torah to adapt to the lives that we would prefer to live—lives in which we do not stone our children to death.

Back to the Middle Path

Somewhere between the path of the rabbis who affirm the Torah while interpreting its meaning to the point of vanishing and the willful and honest "no thank you" of those who allow the sacred texts a vote but not a veto is an attractive middle way. Here we can hope to feel the presence of God, as well as the hand of man, in the Torah while admitting that parts of it do not make moral sense to us.

On this middle path, we can say two contradictory things —first, that we want to find a complete meaning in the Torah that we can endorse and embrace; and second, that, for the moment, some pieces of the text surely do not fit that vision. We find ourselves without a complete answer and with work to do—work in understanding the text and work in understanding our lives. Allowing the Torah a vote is not enough. We do not begin with the idea of human experience coming first and Torah following with a vote, a veto, or follow-on wisdom. Instead, we accept the notion of divinity, and our challenge is to find the true divinity in the Torah, imperfect to our understanding as the Torah may be.

The writer Ilan Stavans offered a lovely exposition of this challenge when he spoke to friends and family from the bimah at his son's bar mitzvah. "The Torah gives us everything," he said. "Not only what is beautiful, but what is ugly too, all of life, all the joys and sorrows, the complications, the expressions, the things we hate and the things we love." His son's Torah portion dealt with bodily fluids and excretions and was a bit much for some. But Stavans's point was that the Torah challenges us in this way as part of its very design: what it contains is not merely the lovely and the wise but also the aweful and the shocking as well, and this is neither an accident nor a relic of a worn-out worldview but instead a challenge to us to engage everything in the world as we frame our lives within the understanding of a wide-reaching creation and divine creator. The challenge here is to move past seeing the Torah as a set of instructions and to see it instead as a version of the world itself that needs to be understood and respected but never mistaken for something simple and straightforward.

To Correct the World

Finding something new in the ancient texts is by no means limited to the more liberal followers of the Torah. Adin Steinsaltz is a widely influential Israeli rabbi who has founded numerous schools and completed an extensive translation of the Talmud from Aramaic to modern Hebrew complete with his own commentary. He has been named by a group of revivalist rabbis as the *nasi*, or ultimate rabbinic leader, of a new Sanhedrin, the religious body charged with overseeing political and communal life in Israel. While the current Sanhedrin is entirely without any practical power, Steinsaltz is a forceful intellectual figure and widely admired in Orthodox communities around the world. He offers a revealing interpretation of the most traditional views of the Torah. "Other religions," he wrote in his book *The Thirteen-Petaled Rose*, "have a concept of spripture as deriving from Heaven, but only Judiasm seems to be based on the idea that the Torah Scripture is itself Heaven. In other words, the Torah of the Jews is the essence of divine revelation; it is not only the basis for social, political, and religious life but is in itself something of supreme value. . . . As the sages have said: before creation, God looked into the Torah and made the world accordingly."

Steinsaltz captures the mystical quality of Torah study that drives so many Orthodox men to devote so many hours and so much of their passion to working with the Jewish scriptures: "The intellectual study of Torah and the emotional involvement in its contents are a form of identification with the divine will, and what may be called God's dream of the existence of the world and the existance of man. One who is immersed in Torah becomes a partner of God, in the sense that man on the one hand and God on the other are participating in the planning, the spinning out of the idea, the common dream of the existence of the world." Still, for traditionalists like Steinsaltz, cocreation has its limits. In his work, he translates "tikkun olam" not as "to heal the world" but as "to *correct* the world." Becoming a partner with God and sharing the common dream of existence is a powerful thing. But it is God's thing first and last, and our cocreation is very much about getting God's will right and not much at all about reimagining or reshaping what that will might be.

Yet Steinsaltz offers a remarkable vision of balance, of leading and being led, in his image of man as a partner of God. Some may argue that the weakness of a rule-driven, spricture-led religious life is that it turns people back to the old texts all the time and prevents them from experiencing that profound face-to-face connection with God. But Steinsaltz clearly sees something different in the heart of Torah. He does not see Torah as the residue of someone else's experience of God, the book that tells the story of other people encountering the divine, but instead as the very place where God and man meet. Look to the texts, he says, with great discipline and over many years, and you do not see the past. Instead, you join in the creation of the future.

Finding the Limits of
Reinterpretation and Reinvention

Recall the thoughts of the Ivy League economist who noted that the "incentives for being Jewish in practical terms are much smaller than the incentives for becoming part of the dominant religion in the larger community most of us live in." One lesson of the emergence of Christianity is that interpretation and addition can lead to wholesale redefinition, to the point that Judiasm is no longer Judaism and that the Jew is no longer a Jew. The movement from Judaism to Christianity can be portrayed as a loss, or even a tragedy; but it is also portrayed by many millions of people as the fulfilment of the incomplete promise of the old Judiasm and as the expression of the full universalism that philosopher Michael Walzer, among so many other Jews, hopes to find in the Torah.

If we do not recognize some limits on interpretation and reimagining of the Torah, then the Judaism that survives may well not be Judaism at all. This risk might be necessary to make the engagement with Torah truly meaningful to a wide population, but the risk is enormous. It is, ultimately, the same challenge as demography: do we want to count how many or how deeply Jewish the Jewish people are? Do we want the Torah to have the greatest possible number of followers or followers in the truest possible spirit of what the Torah is? This is not a question with a universal answer, but the character of the Jewish future will depend on how we choose to answer it.

So where do we draw the line? How much reinterpretation of the Torah is enough, and how much is too much? This question emerges early, in the figure of Moses and the idea of the "oral law," or "oral Torah."

"All the commandments were given to Moses at Saini," Maimonides wrote in the opening line of his enormously influential twelfth-century collection of rabbinic writings and law, the *Mishneh Torah*, and they

were given together with their interpretation, as it is written "And I will give you tablets of stone, and the Law, and the Commandment." (Exod. 24:12) "Law" is the written law, and "Commandment" is its interpretation; we were commanded to fulfill the Law, according to the Commandment. And the Commandment is what we call the Oral Law. . . . The whole of the Law was written down by Moshe our teacher before his death, in his own hand. . . . But the Commandment which is the interpretation of the Law—he did not write it down, but gave orders concerning it to the elders, to Yeheshua, and to all the rest of Israel.

From rabbi to rabbi, generation to generation, this oral law was passed on, and after the destruction of the Second Temple in 70 CE, was codified in the Mishnah, the center of the Talmud, about 200 CE.

The oral law, or oral Torah, elevated the rabbinic function: unlike religions in which the priestly class guides followers in understanding sacred texts and teachings that exist on their own terms, in Judaism the rabbis according to this teaching had access to a divine law that their followers did not. The rabbis themselves contained secret and divine texts. From a purely sociological view, this makes the priestly class doubly powerful. They not only serve a sacred function, but they are themselves the vessels of sacred, secret knowledge. Rabbis could win any argument against a noncleric, because the rabbis could claim recourse to oral law, the body of knowledge transmitted by Moses but transmitted only to rabbis—so the rabbis know it and the laity don't. The creation of the Talmud helped to soften this imbalance. Through the Talmud, rabbinic wisdom is now available for any scholar with the time and intellect to puzzle out the elegant, complex volumes of commentary, and Maimonides takes the distillation of these debates to a level of greater clarity in his *Mishneh Torah*, the very purpose of which was to make the heart of the collected rabbinic teachings more accessible.

How striking—and how characteristically Jewish—that even this source of special rabbinic knowledge and privilege is all about commentary and interpretation. Oral law as laid out in the *Mishneh* and explicated by Maimonides refers back to the five books of Moses constantly. But as almost any reader will notice, this explication makes the original text more complex and harder to understand, rather than simpler and more accessible. The Talmud does not take us to new places but more deeply into the places where we already are and have been.

■

In Deuteronomy, Moses tells the Jewish people that they will live with great prosperity, "if thou shalt hearken to the voice of the LORD thy God, to keep his commandments and statutes." And doing so, Moses continues,

is not too hard for thee, neither is it far off.

It is not in heaven, that thou shouldst say: "Who shall go up to heaven, and bring it unto us, and make us to hear it, that we may do it?"

Neither is it beyond the sea, that thou shouldst say: "Who shall go over the sea for us, and bring it unto us, and make us to hear it, that we may do it?"

But the word is very nigh unto thee, in thy mouth, and in thy heart, that thou mayest do it. (Deut. 30:10–14)

Do not look for another prophet, Moses seems to say—you do not need another man to climb a mountain on your behalf to find the truth of God, because your prophet has already come and God's wisdom is already with you, even inside you. All you must do now is follow it.

"There is a story in the Talmud," writes Walter Kaufmann, "in which some rabbis have an argument about a point of law. One of them performs various miracles to persuade the others that he is right, and when all else fails he exclaims: 'If the law is as I think, they shall tell us from heaven.' And a loud voice is heard: 'What have you against Rabbi Eliezer, for the law is as he says.' But the rabbis decide: 'We no longer pay attention to voices, for on Mount Sinai already thou hast written into the Torah to decide according to the majority.'"

Why no longer listen to the voices from heaven? Because by this time in the history of Judaism, new prophetic voices would change the rules of a game already codified and functioning well according to the laws laid down by Moses. New prophets put everything back in play and threaten not only the spiritual but also the material substance of Judaism. New prophets could make Judaism into something else—and indeed, new prophets *have* taken the foundation of Judaism and made new religions from it, most notably Christianity and Islam, just as the new prophets of these religions made out of mainstream American Protestantism new religions like Mormonism and the faith of the Jehovah's Witnesses as well as the faith of the Sufis and the Nation of Islam.

Prophecy brings a new word from God and always threatens the received status quo. If we want the kind of change in Judaism that might make it more meaningful and real in the lives of ordinary Jewish people today, but without making something fundamentally new and different from the Judiasm we have inherited, we might simply say that many new aspects to Judaism might be good, except for new prophecy. We can say that we want a new approach to the core of Judaism but that we do not want new prophets, to give us a new Torah or a new religion. New prophecy may well be the precise point at which we recognize that we are leaving behind Judaism as we understand it.

Certainly the books of the Prophets, which we now include as the second of the three sections of the Jewish scriptures, had an enormous effect on the Judaism that had come before them—the Judaism that we see so vividly portrayed in the five books of Moses. Is this a different religion—because of its new prophets—or an extension of the old? The only way to answer this question is to read the five books of Moses and to ask whether the Judaism there—filled with revelation and struggle, with mystical vision and the creation of a people—is the same Judaism we practice today. In some ways the answer is yes, but in many ways not. The religion of the Prophets, affirmed and declaimed by their twentieth-century emissary Abraham Joshua Heschel, is in some ways closer to what one might find in most congregations. Certainly there are several different Judaisms, from the named and known movements, ranging from Haredi Orthodox and Jewish Renewal, to the communities meeting quietly and crafting their own visions that we will know about in a decade if they survive and grow. Are these different religions? Perhaps as different as the Church of Jesus Christ of the Latter Day Saints is from Catholicism, or as different as the Nation of Islam is from the Koranic Muslim mainstream. When the followers of hard-core, five-books Orthodoxy look at

Conservative and Reform synagogues and declare them not truly Jewish, they present a compelling answer. Mainstream Judaism today is different from the Judaism that drew a line after Deuteronomy and said, in effect, stop looking for a new word from God. The Judaism of compassion, the Judiasm of tikkun olam, the Judaism that does not stone its disobediant children and kill everything that breathes in the villages of its apostates and enemies, is something different; and if it did not exist, the end of Judaism would be far closer than it is today.

Of course, this leaves most contemporary Jews in an uncomfortable place. We say, thank God Judaism has evolved past that starting point. And new prophecy is what made that evolution happen. But we also say that in order to remain Jewish, we don't want to follow new prophets from this point forward. We find ourselves in the position of so many generations, saying that the change that got us *here* was great but the change that might take us somewhere new is not so kosher. Reason won't take us beyond this point, but faith and feeling might leave us comfortably in this position of contraditction, noting that it makes no sense but gives us what we need: the Torah; lives in the mainstream of the societies we inhabit; and an itchy feeling that we can and should strive to do a little better, that we have not quite arrived, and that our goodness is likely not quite good enough, so we need to keep working to knit together our ethical, communal, and social lives, which have not yet come fully together.

Putting In and Taking Out from the Scrolls

Rabbi Naomi Levy was one of the first women to graduate from the Jewish Theological Seminary. She became a rabbi in California and not long ago published a book in which she told about the day after Yom Kippur a few years ago. A woman, a congregant at Levy's shul, arrived at the temple door that day, her face bruised. She told Levy how sorry she was to have missed Yom Kippur services. She could not attend, she said, because she'd been the victim of a crime, beaten and brutalized. Levy talked with her, prayed with her, and then opened the ark of the Torah, took the scrolls out, and brought them to the injured woman, who held them and continued to pray. The woman felt transformed, strengthened by the scrolls.

What gave her that strength? Was it the words of the Torah—the presence of God there? Was it the human history of those scrolls—the fact that her father and her father's father and back again generations, all read these words, held these scrolls or scrolls like them? In shul, when the scrolls pass in the aisle, congregants reach toward them. On the bimah, the honored readers kiss their prayer shawls and touch them to the scrolls—these are sacred objects. But does that sacredness come from the scrolls or from the people who invest their faith in them?

Dayenu—it would be enough—if these scrolls were our sources of power and faith because in them we can find our fathers and mothers, we can find Moses and Sarah and the Jews of Egypt and the Jews of Poland and the Jews of the camps and the Jews of the new world, the lost Jews and the free Jews, our families for a thousand generations back. It would be enough to take our strength from the Torah only because our history is there and because the hearts and souls of generations of our families are there. But many people see more, as well. They see the joining of humanity and divinity that Adin Seinsaltz describes.

Personally, I believe that there is more in the scrolls than the human community the scrolls represent. And I belive that there is more in the scrolls than merely the ideas of the sacred, in the abstract aspects of the words inscribed there. The most transcendant aspects of the Torah to me are at first human and humane; I am awed by the human history (in some ways, my family history) that has revolved around the scrolls for thousands of years. But I also recognize a divine presence in and through the lives of these people. For me, the scrolls lead to the people; the people lead to God. My bottom-line understanding is that the Torah's meaning is not absolute and unwavering but that it is also never entirely up to us to invent. It is put there by the woman in Rabbi Levy's congregation, by the Jews of Egypt and Poland, the ancient Jews, the Jews of the camps, and the Jews of my boyhood—by the generations of our fathers and mothers, as they have lived their lives of suffering and joy as they have beheld God. Whether I choose to nor not, I feel the divine and the sacred in the Torah, but, as Heschel argued, never without the presence of others beside me.

The limit on interpretation, for me, is the point at which I lose this communal presence as I read and consider the Torah. If I interpret it to the point that its message is no longer of and for Jews specifically—even as it might embrace others and, I hope, even as it recognizes the equal presciousness to God of all humanity—then I have gone too far.

I acknowledge that in the five books of Moses there are demands explicit enough that I am indeed saying no to them as I live my life a step away from the literalism of Torah. I recognize as well that the Prophets, the Writings, and all the rabbinical dialogue and debate that follow do not allow me quite enough cover to make this personal choice and still claim to be a direct and literal follower of the Torah's commands. I've opted for some degree of compromise but only up to a point, within a boundary. I retain a commitment to the teachings of the Torah that prevent a Jew from becoming something else—that's my boundary. And I suspect that it is an important one for many other Jews as well.

Something Unexpected

Nowhere is that edge between being a Jew and not quite being one more fully mapped and explored than in the history of the Reform movement. The story of Reform Judaism suggests something unexpected to those not steeped in its institutional history. The most traditional, explicitly demanding modes of Jewish worship shelter under the umbrella of Orthodox Judaism, and it makes a certain amount of sense to assume that these gave way at some point to the Conservative movement, less demanding and less separatist, and that then as time passed, Conservatism begat Reform, the most tolerant and "progressive" of the three principal strands of Judaism and the one that now claims about 40 percent of all affiliated Jews in the United States, the largest share by far. But this is not at all what happened.

Orthodoxy itself, the sprawling collection of traditional Judaisms from around the world, did not exist as such until the middle of the nineteenth century, when assimilated German Jews chose to mark their territory by formalizing a new way to be a Jew—a way that would soften the social differences between Jews and others and that would make the synagogue look and feel a good bit more like Protestant Christian houses of worship, shifting, for example, the day of prayer from Saturday to Sunday. The movement that had begun in Germany took greater root in the United States as late nineteenth-century congregations chose the Reform path, congregation by congregation. The Reform movement here coalesced and issued its Pittsburgh Platform in 1885.

That document tries to reinvent Judaism. "We recognize in every religion," it says, "an attempt to grasp the Infinite, and in every mode, source or book of revelation held sacred in any religious system the consciousness of the indwelling of God in man. We hold that Judaism presents the highest conception of the God-idea as taught in our Holy Scriptures and developed and spiritualized by the Jewish teachers, in accordance with the moral and philosophical progress of their respective ages."

It continues, "We recognize in the Mosaic legislation a system of training the Jewish people for its mission during its national life in Palestine, and today we accept as binding only its moral laws, and maintain only such ceremonies as elevate and sanctify our lives, but reject all such as are not adapted to the views and habits of modern civilization." Reform Judaism, as a movement, will take the Torah and use the parts that fit the lives and societies of its followers, while putting aside the parts that do not fit.

In 1937 a restatement of Reform beliefs in the Columbus Platform explained that "as a depository of permanent spiritual ideals, the Torah remains the dynamic source of the life of Israel. Each age has the obligation to adapt the teachings of the Torah to its basic needs in consonance with the genius of Judaism." Here, the basic needs of the age—what could they be?—take some precedence over at least the external details of Torah. The Torah itself is a "depository" of ideals and not God's word or will. The ideals deposited in the Torah will be sorted through; and useful, fit-for-our-age ideals will be made central, the others discarded or kept on the shelf. Mostly it will be the Torah that will be adapted to fit the lived experience of Jews, rather than the other way around.

Not until 1999 when the Reform movement formally ac-

knowledged fundamental changes in the religious experience
and spiritual desires of Reform congregants did this balance
officially shift—and then it shifted in a major way. Back
again in Pittsburgh, the movement's leaders created a new
platform, the first to incorporate Hebrew language and the
first to suggest that the Torah ought to some significant degree be the transformer and we the transformed.

"We hope to transform our lives," the 1999 Pittsburgh
platform said, "through קְדֻשָּׁה (kedushah), holiness." The
new platform goes on to speak directly of God, not of "the
God-idea" as the first Pittsburgh platform did, but of God
the giver of meaning and purpose:

We affirm the reality and oneness of God, even as we may differ
in our understanding of the Divine presence.

We affirm that the Jewish people is bound to God by an eternal
בְּרִית (b'rit), covenant, as reflected in our varied understandings of
Creation, Revelation and Redemption.

We affirm that every human being is created בְּצֶלֶם אֱלֹהִים (b'tzelem
Elohim), in the image of God, and that therefore every human life
is sacred.

We regard with reverence all of God's creation and recognize our
human responsibility for its preservation and protection.

**In all these ways and more, God gives meaning and purpose to
our lives.**

The new platform also speaks directly to the Torah: "We
affirm that Torah is the foundation of Jewish life. We cherish
the truths revealed in Torah, God's ongoing revelation to our
people and the record of our people's ongoing relationship
with God. We affirm that Torah is a manifestation of עוֹלָם
אַהֲבַת (ahavat olam), God's eternal love for the Jewish people

and for all humanity." This is a dramatic step away from the 1885 document, in which the word Torah was never mentioned.

The Reform movement was born among Jews who were troubled that their sacred traditions kept them too far removed from the mainstream experiences of the societies they lived in—Christian Germany and Christian America. A hundred years later, the movement was reshaped by a Jewish American generation that was obviously in the mainstream of American life but without a strong vision of divinity and holiness in their official stance toward Judaism.

This new generation stepped out of its received view that the Torah should be adapted to the world, and created a platform for a greater humility and awe in the face of divinity. Reform is still not a rule-driven movement, but it no longer defines itself in reference to the rules and rituals of Judaism that it rejects. Without the easy notions of modernizing Judaism at its center and with a greater degree of focus on Torah and God, the Reform movement has become spiritually deeper and more demanding of its followers. Reform today claims less for human understanding, more for the mystery of the divine, and makes more allowance for the feeling that religion is a mysterious, inspired path. Not knowing exactly where it leads, and not knowing precisely why, might be part of the wholeness of religious experience that its followers have so strongly wanted.

The Individual Conscience

Not knowing is, in some important ways, the center of all religious experience, and Reform in recent years has become more of a religion than it was at its inception. Reform Judaism is now less of an ethnic, social, and civic institution and

less of a common-interest group. It is now more of a path—
one built on tradition—to encounter God.

Reconstruction has followed a similar path, from Judaism
as a civilization or a society to a new, Torah-centered, more
religious version of itself. The Orthodox and Conservative
movements reveal less of an evolution in their sense of Torah
and God. From their perspectives, this is largely because they
never took the steps away from the central religious experience of Judaism that were the very origin of the Reform and
Reconstruction movements. But this is too simple and avoids
the enormous leap that Judaism has taken, through the Reform movement especially, beyond a rule-driven worship and
toward an engagement with the conscience of the modern
individual who hopes to arrive at a rich and deep Jewish experience as a matter of personal faith and not as a matter of
commandment, obedience, or covenant.

This broadening of concern takes the name of the collectivity of the Jewish people—Israel, literally "those who
wrestle with God"—to a more fundamental starting point
than most Orthodox or Conservative thinkers are comfortable with, not only wrestling with God and the Torah but
with the self as it approaches God and the Torah. The starting point here is not in the middle of the story—where we
would wake and find ourselves Jews, part of a people and a
congregation with our true and perfect sacred text in front of
us—but at the beginning: we wake and have every option, to
belong or not to belong, to believe or not to believe, to approach the Torah or to leave it aside.

At the bar mitzvah of a friend's son recently, I sat in awe
as three generations of the young man's relatives, men and
women, were called to the Torah and read in flawless, lyri-
cal Hebrew from the scrolls, their voices colored by hints
of English, Spanish, and Polish, but each offering clear, profound ancient Hebrew. I told my friend how impressed I was,

and he modestly replied, "Well, we all were forced to go to the Hebrew and Yiddish day schools for our whole child-hoods—we had to learn this." Without that "have to," most don't, and then we sit in shul feeling excluded—called inwardly to pray, but not really knowing how.

Judaism has always put an emphasis on community, making shared human experience an essential and unavoidable path for connection to God, as opposed to emphasizing the individual's direct, unmediated contact with the divine. Judaism is not a religion in which one can sin against his neighbor and then look to God—rather than the neighbor—for forgiveness. Doing and feeling, action and belief, are tightly bound together, and belief does not trump lived experience. The connection to Jewish learning is clear: if we dwell too much on the struggle of faith before we approach Torah, we may have too little time in the end for the great learning that opens so many Jewish—and human—pathways.

Writer David Gelernter draws an important parallel: "Theology," he writes, "in general is less central to Judaism than to the other great religions. Practice, the rabbis insist, comes first; illumination later. (In the words of a midrash, 'Let a man first do good deeds, and then ask God for knowledge of Torah; let a man first act as the righteous and the upright act, and then let him ask God for wisdom; let a man first grasp the way of humility, and then ask God for understanding')."

If we wait to learn Hebrew and the prayers and to study the Talmud until we feel called to faith, we might wait until we have no time for serious study in our lives as workers, parents, friends, and neighbors. There is simply so much to learn.

This sense of frustration was a large part of the motive of the Reform's early turn away from Hebrew—to pull down the barrier for those who are not educated like European ye-shiva buchers with the languages and the texts in their heads and on their tongues—to let more Jewish people further into the center of Jewish worship. But the verdict on the decades of this way of being Jewish is clear: pulling down the barriers, the movement also compromised what was on the other side. The movement made entry into Jewish worship easier, but it also simultaneously demoted God from *Eyeh Asher Eyeh* to "the God-idea." If the mainstreams of Conservatism and Orthodoxy did not make this same mistake through most of the past hundred years, they also did not do much to address the daunting barriers at all—except, perhaps, to affirm them and to hold fast to a Judaism that cherishes its obscurities and apartness.

Reform and Reconstruction—as well as some of the less central strands of the Conservative and Orthodox movements—have done something far more profound. They have accepted the challenge of the Enlightenment and the philosophical individualism of the modern West and struggled with how to reconcile that with the spiritual heart of Judaism. They have gone out from the walls surrounding Torah to engage the wandering Jewish soul and to wander with it, at times away from tradition and at times back toward it—changed by their journeys, still speaking a language more recognizable to the average Jewish man or woman in the twenty-first century than that of Conservatism or Orthodoxy, but more explicitly focused now on Torah and on what God will become. The center of the mainstream of modern Judaism has found a middle path, and this is a cause of great hope.

Conservative rabbi Menahem Creditor speaks directly to this point, thinking about the institutional path of Conservatism. "Our progressive/halachic blend can be both seductive and compelling, and our decisions should be celebrated as steps forward. . . . The 'middle road' can also lead to God. We just need to decide it's our destination." The evolution of the three major non-Orthodox movements—Reform, Conservatism, and Reconstruction—seems in the past generation to follow just that path, from the "God-idea" to God, from civilization to divinity, and from a sense of Judaism as a fact of identity to more a matter of faith.

■

If Judaism is to have a meaningful future even in the face of stagnant or declining demographics, that future will certainly be a result of faith rather than fertility, of our connection to divinity rather than the strength of our borders both material and figurative. A more numerous Judaism, a better defended Judaism, and a more militant Judaism do not speak to Heschel's question of whether we are living for the sake of heaven, the best and most Jewish question to hold in mind as we consider the future of the Jewish people.

To Heschel, the book of Ecclesiastes offers a balancing thought—with its distinctive flavor of wisdom and charm—that speaks directly to the future of the Jews. "For to him that is joined to all the living there is hope," we are told, "for a living dog is better than a dead lion." Survival matters. "For the living know that they shall die; but the dead know not any thing, neither have they any more a reward; for the memory of them is forgotten" (Eccl. 9:4–5).

These are the poles between which we will transit the decades and centuries to come: to live for the sake of heaven and to survive. When one dominates the other, we will need to set the balance right again. Without that balance, the Jewish people will either cease to be truly Jewish or will cease to be.

Jews for What?

For many mainstream Jews, "Jews for Jesus" is a convenient label for all ethnically Jewish people who worship in Christian churches or accept Jesus as the Messiah. More specifically, Jews for Jesus is a thirty-year-old San Francisco–based nonprofit organization that operates like many Christian ministries. It reported to the federal government that among its principal accomplishments in the year 2007,

1. We saw 813 people come to the Lord, including 591 Jewish people.
2. We had personal contact with 12,201 people who expressed an interest in finding out more about our message. We completed 11,485 personal visits with people.
3. We hand delivered 3,627,000 gospel tracts on the streets.

While the appeal of Christian belief and worship is hard to ignore in a country that is overwhelmingly Christian, and while Christian belief and worship certainly have inherent merits, the specific tactics of the San Francisco group—targeting cities with large Jewish populations, fishing for new adherents—are roundly and often angrily rejected by most Jewish leaders and organizations. The Jewish Community Relations Council of New York addresses Jews for Jesus through its Spiritual Deception Prevention Project (a project formerly called the Task Force on Missionaries and Cults).

In a *New York Times* article covering a 2006 outreach program on the streets of Manhattan, Craig Miller, a staffer at the Spiritual Deception Prevention Project, summed up his group's position: "This is not Jewish versus Christian. It's about deception pure and simple. The groups that are coming are bringing a deceptive message that one can be both Christian and part of the Jewish community." Scott Hillman—head of a group formed to counter Jews for Jesus, called Jews for Judaism—presented his group's outlook to the *Washington Post* in 2007: "You don't dress up fundamentalist, evangelical Christian missionaries in Jewish clothing and call it Judaism."

And these are the calmer opponents of Jews for Jesus. Follow the outreach staff of Jews for Jesus on the streets of New York or Los Angeles, and you'll see clusters of people surround them, doing everything they can to stop the group's work. Why? Because this not-for-profit group is such a vivid symbol of Jews and Judaism fading away, becoming a chapter in the history of another religion that wishes to swallow it whole.

Theory J

Call it Theory J of the future of the Jewish people: the most popular variation on the spiritual argument that the number of Jews does not matter, but the quality of Jews is the real issue, and even one single Jew, if he or she is fully, deeply, and transcendently Jewish is better than millions of Jews without that kind of spiritual substance. This argument captures the faith-versus-logic essence of so much of religious thought and distills the personal spiritual struggle to connect with divinity and live a righteous life. It makes religion and God personal and allows us to put aside the worldly affairs of institutional and communal religion to focus more on the heavenly business to be done. And yet the one-great-Jew outlook is, from another perspective, the story of Christianity. To his followers, Jesus is the greatest Jew, the perfect Jew. His existence answers all questions; in him and through him alone, salvation is real and is universally available. This terrifies many Jews when they consider the future of their religion. It has already proven a powerful path toward the end of the Jewish story.

Jesus certainly thought of himself as a Jew, and there are many millions of Christians who frame their faith as the extension and perfection of Judaism. And so this is one end point, one theory, of what will become of the Jews: Judaism will be remembered, invoked, and celebrated as the starting point of Christianity, of Islam, and of other Abrahamic religions yet to come. Judaism will be invoked, and perhaps every Christian and Muslim will feel just a little bit Jewish. But Judaism as an active faith will be gone.

Theory Z

The first photograph in this book offers a different theory of the future. Call it Theory Z: like the Zoroastrians, another group that does not proselytize and demands lineal parentage within the faith, Jews will largely vanish, recalled by scholars, perhaps flickering in remnant congregations here and there but more as curiosities than anything else. Christianity and Islam will come to speak less and less of Judaism, except as a false start or a corrupt understanding of a truth beyond its grasp. Theory Z does not require Christians to convert Jews or Nazis to exterminate Jews or other avowed enemies of the Jewish people to do much of anything at all. It is the structure of the religion itself that predicts its end.

Because like Zoroastrianism Judaism does not proselytize and because like Zoroastrianism it requires lineal descent from one parent (for Zoroastrianism, the father; for Judaism, the mother), it is not suited to a cosmopolitan world. Its boundaries seem built to keep strangers out; and in a world that invites and celebrates boundary crossing, Jews leave the inner circle with ease while others are barred from entering.

And like Zoroastrians, Jews share the demographic downside of their cultural strength—they are relatively prosperous, they are relatively well educated, and they are relatively egalitarian in the roles women are allowed and encouraged to play. These traits, across every culture in the world, lead to smaller family size. Theory Z suggests that these facts of what Judaism is, rather than what others do to Judaism and Jews, will bring its demise.

∎

These are dark scenarios and perhaps too extreme—or too long in their making—to feel like prophecies we ought to, or can, do much about today. And if they are true, there is not much to be done to fight them. Theory J is in essence a spiritual prediction, not a practical one. And Theory Z hinges on Judaism's essential traits. To fight Theory Z, we would need Judaism to become, in effect, a different kind of religion—fulfilling its prophecy of doom even as we fight it.

Theory Five and the Prophetic Future

But there are two other scenarios worth considering, both just as likely as J and Z, and both closer to the lived experience of many Jews today. They demand closer thought because they are not, on their own terms, unstoppable or inevitable.

The first might be called Theory Five: the tough and at times exclusionary worldview of Jews as God's Holy Nation, without peers, expressed in the five books of Moses.

The second might be called the Prophetic Future: the Judaism of the five books of Moses called to account by the prophets and forced into fiery dialogue with its emerging generations. This Judaism is subject to revision while still bounded by great commitment to Jewish identity and faith in a specifically Jewish God. This is the Judaism of Heschel, with the five books of Moses demanding deep commitment to the Jewish nation and with the books of the Prophets demanding just as deep a commitment to everyone else.

■

The first two visions of the future, Theories J and Z, are easily arrived at, and we may well be on our irrevocable way to either one. They are the result of passivity, of the acquiescence to Judaism's millennia-long arc from minor cult to foundational faith and, perhaps, back to where it began.

The other two visions of the future are far more interesting. They both presume that Jews wish to defend Judaism and the idea of Jews as a living people, but each presumes a different motive. On the one hand, we can defend Judaism and the Jewish people because we are special, different, and privileged by God to sit nearer to him—in which case the logic of separation in every aspect of life, from the politics of nations to the politics of education and the politics of the silverware, becomes compelling. Indeed, this is a wonderfully logical position. We have the five books of Moses that tell us rather clearly how special we are; and if we confine our studies and arguments to parsing the shades of meaning in that wonderful and self-satisfying message, we can live deeply committed lives as Jews with strong borders of every kind surrounding us.

Or we can turn the page to read the prophets and hear their challenge. Here the logic collapses—we are special, but everyone is special too. Our special status uplifts us but makes us only more equal and more burdened with the well-being of others. To be whole ourselves, in our minority community, we have to heal the world at large. To go inward, we have to look outward. It does not, in fact, make much literal sense—but it speaks to the economist who pointed out that being Jewish at all in this world is not much a matter of sense but of faith and feeling.

■

I wrote a number of the early pages of this book in the airport in Birmingham, Alabama, waiting for a delayed flight back to New York. I lived nearby, with my wife and my daughters and my son.

I began writing this book after I had been accepted to rabbinical seminary but decided not to go. The book became something of an outlet for my long consideration of Jewish identity and my personal role as a Jew in a world that was alternately welcoming and hostile to my people. My father was, at the time, near the end of a long illness. As I've said earlier, it became more and more clear to me as he aged—as I aged—that being a Jew was the anchor of his identity. He died while I wrote the book.

About a year before his passing, when his mind was still relatively sharp, I asked him a question I'd thought of a thousand times: when you look back at your life, why do you think you've been so angry so often? He looked surprised. Angry? Him? Why would I think of such a thing?

It was a little like the boy with chocolate batter covering his face asking why in the world we might think he'd eaten the brownie mix. My father had indeed been an angry man, and no doubt the reasons for his anger were varied and substantial. Among them was his experience as a Jew. His feelings as a boy, hearing the news of the Holocaust, left deep marks. He could choke up talking about Hitler and the Nazis. He could pound the table. He could fill so thoroughly with righteous fury that he seemed to be a man on fire.

It took me a long time to feel Jewish history so personally. Perhaps it is an inheritance, a bequeathal from my father. He has left me some of his Jewish anger, and I do feel it now. A man on the street in Los Angeles, where I live today, makes a bullying gesture toward two Jews in black hats and fringes, and I pull my car over ready to leap out, my blood boiling. The man is gone by the time I open my door, and I stand down. But this is my father's anger, and I suspect it was his father's and his father's before him.

Do I want it to be my son's anger as well?

My son's bar mitzvah turned out to be a fairly conventional affair, no American Indian vision quest, no turning of his back on the religion of our family and our faith. Our ceremony was presided over by a young rabbi without a congregation. She is only twenty-six, rides a motorcycle, and wrote her rabbinical thesis on what she views as the misreading of the Torah as it applies to tattoos. She's in favor and has more than one.

In his speech to our family and friends, my son said this: "For me, the center of Judaism is discussion—strong opinions, strong feelings, sometimes being hurt, sometimes being healed, not simply agreeing for the sake of agreement, but going beyond the false idea that we all agree, that we've already reached the important conclusions and settled on the meanings of things."

I helped him a little, but this is his take on how it feels to be a Jew. I think he hit the mark pretty well. We have to fight our way to the meaning of our faith; we have to remake it again and again and again. Our heritage is truly not anger but struggle, not a set of laws but the imperative to make and remake a body of wisdom for our people that will guide us, keep us whole, and help us make our way through a sometimes mysterious world.

We were asked to provide some lines of poetry for the pamphlet of prayers prepared for all our son's bar mitzvah guests. We chose these, by Charles Reznikoff:

Day after day in the wilderness,
year after year,
until you see a bush burning.
Yes, but you have to climb a mountain
to speak with God.

My son's point seems to be that our religion is about the climbing of the mountain at least as much as it is about talking with God. Or to take a step further, with Abraham Joshua Heschel's words about "praying with our feet" in mind, perhaps climbing the mountain is itself a way to talk with God.

The easiest cliché seems the truest: it's all about the journey. Or as my son has said, it's all about the discussion. Recall that when we get the translation right, our God is the God of becoming, the God whose name is "I will be who I will be."

■

I think again of that imaginary rabbi, infinitely wise. We put to this rabbi a question, *the* question: "Is the proper Jewish path the one that leads back to the Jewish center or the path that leads out into the world?"

And with a smile, he gives the most important answer: "Yes."

Notes

2. How Much Change Can Judaism Stand?

18 **"Thou hast ordained"**: This section of Psalm 119, along with all following text from the Hebrew Bible unless otherwise noted, comes from the Jewish Publication Society's 1917 translation.

20 **"a single truth"**: Samuel C. Heilman, "Jews and Fundamentalism," *Journal of Ecumenical Studies* 42, no. 1 (Winter 2007): 29–41, 29.

21 **"fundamentals of the faith"**: Heilman, "Jews and Fundamentalism."

22 **"exaltation and awe"**: Arthur Green, "God, Prayer, and Religious Language," in *Imagining the Jewish Future: Essays and Responses*, ed. David A. Teutsch (Albany: State University of New York Press, 1992), 13–22, 13.

25 **"book of Exodus"**: Steven M. Cohen and Jack Wertheimer, "Whatever Happened to the Jewish People" *Commentary* 121, no. 6 (2006): 33–37.

25 **"price for freedom"**: Hannah Arendt, *Essays in Understanding, 1930–1954: Formation, Exile, and Totalitarianism* (New York: Harcourt Brace, 1994), 18.

26 **"Mounting evidence"**: Cohen and Wertheimer, "Whatever Happened to the Jewish People" 33.

3. The First and Second Photographs

45 **"it is Jewish"**: Leon Wieseltier, "Because They Believe," review of *Why Are Jews Liberal*, by Podhoretz, *New York Times*, September 13, 2009.

45 "**survival** *as what?*": Marshall Meyer, "Congregation B'Nai Jeshurun: The Power of a Relevant Message," in *Church and Synagogue Affiliation: Theory, Research and Practice,* ed. Amy L. Sales and Gary A. Tobin (Westport CT: Greenwood Press, 1995), 143–51, 150.

47 "**scrupulous and unremitting inquiry**": John Dewey, *Reconstruction in Philosophy* (New York: Henry Holt, 1920), 165.

48 **an affliction:** Mordechai M. Kaplan, *Judaism as a Civilization: Towards a Reconstruction of American-Jewish Life* (New York: Macmillan, 1934), 3.

48 **The Past Has a Vote:** Jewish Reconstructionist Federation, "Who Is a Reconstructionist Jew?" Jewish Reconstructionist Federation, http://jrf.org/showres&rid=140 (accessed October 16, 2007).

49 "**different from traditional Judaism**": Lester Bronstein, "What Is Reconstructionist Judaism?" http://www.rrc.edu/resources/reconstructionist-resource/what-reconstructionist-judaism?print=1 (accessed December 3, 2011).

50 "**Torah as . . . response**": Bronstein, "What Is Reconstructionist Judaism?"

50 "**primary respondents**": Bronstein, "What Is Reconstructionist Judaism?"

50 "**God does not choose**": Bronstein, "What Is Reconstructionist Judaism?"

51 "**rooted in . . . traditions**": Mary Butler, "Kabbalah Consciousness," http://www.ricktoss.com/references/kabbalah/kabbalah90.html (accessed December 4, 2011).

51 "**sacred purpose**": "About ALEPH," http://www.aleph.org/about.htm (accessed December 4, 2011).

55 "**Are ye not as**": This translation is the Jewish Publication Society's 1917 text. In a 1989 lecture at Oxford University on this topic, Walzer used the King James translation, the word order of which varies in only one instance. In his 2001 lecture at the Carnegie Council on Ethics in International Affairs, "Universalism and Jewish Values," which is the focus

of my comments above, Walzer offers the strikingly different 1985 Jewish Publication Society translation:

To Me, O Israelites, you are
Just like the Ethiopians
—declares the Lord.
True, I brought Israel up
From the land of Egypt,
But also the Philistines from Caphtor
And the Arameans from Kir.

55 **"The Torah commands"**: Rabbi Abraham Isaac Kook, *In the Desert a Vision*, trans. Bezalel Naor (Spring Valley: Orot, 2000), 44–45.

56 **"THE JEWISH PEOPLE"**: Rabbi Meir Kehane, "The Authentic Jewish Idea: Policies and Programs," http://clubmaoz.org/authentic_jewish_idea.htm (accessed December 4, 2011).

57 **"obedience to that Law"**: Kehane, "The Authentic Jewish Idea."

67 **"more broad-minded"**: Jahangir Pocha, "Shrinking Population Threatens an Ancient Faith," *Boston Globe*, September 5, 2004, http://www.boston.com/news/world/articles/2004/09/05/shrinking-population-threatens-an-ancient-faith?pg-full (accessed December 4, 2011).

69 **"We have a responsibility"**: Rana Rosen, "Zoroastrians, Divided over Commissions, Face a Shrinking Future," Religion News Service, March 27, 2007. Reprinted at http://religionblog.dallasnews.com/archives/2007/3/zoroastrianism-a-to-z.html.

71 **"the years of exile"**: Peter Clark, *Zoroastrianism: An Introduction to an Ancient Faith* (Eastbourne, U.K.: Sussex Academic Press, 1998), 152.

4. The Third Photograph

77 **"Let us do our thinking"**: Walter Rauschenbusch, *Christianity and the Social Crisis* (New York: Macmillan, 1908), xv.

77 **"every religious man"**: Rauschenbusch, *Christianity and the Social Crisis*, 2.

78 **"religion and ethics are inseparable"**: Rauschenbusch, *Christianity and the Social Crisis*, 7.

78 **"injustice is here"**: Martin Luther King Jr., "Letter from a Birmingham Jail," April 16, 1963, King Center, Atlanta GA, found online at *H-Net: Humanities and Social Sciences Online*, http://www.h-net.org/~hst306/documents/letter.html.

81 **"Tell your brother"**: Seth Cagin and Philip Dray, *We Are Not Afraid: The Story of Goodman, Schwerner and Chaney, and the Civil Rights Campaign for Mississippi* (New York: Scribner, 1988), 308.

81 **"bunch of chimpanzees"**: Jere Nash and Andy Taggart, *Mississippi Politics: The Struggle for Power, 1976–2008* (Jackson: University Press of Mississippi, 2009), 112.

81 **"My husband . . . did not die in vain"**: Jewish Women's Archive, "Rita Schwerner Statement to Newspapers on the Discovery of Her Husband's Body on 4th August, 1964," http://jwa.org/media/rita-schwerner-statement-to-newspapers-on-discovery-of-her-husband's-body-on-4th-august-1964 (accessed December 4, 2011).

83 **"The traditional Torah"** Kaplan, *Judaism as a Civilization*, 414.

83 **"Prophecy is a reminder"**: Abraham Joshua Heschel, *The Prophets* (New York: Harper Row, 1962), 297.

83 **"God's life"**: Heschel, *The Prophets*, 297.

84 **"Prayer is meaningless"**: Abraham Joshua Heschel, *Moral Grandeur and Spiritual Audacity: Essays* (New York: Farrar, Straus, and Giroux, 1996), 262.

88 **"Our aim"**: Roy Reel, "25,000 Go to Alabama's Capitol," *New York Times*, March 25, 1965, 1.

88 **"At the first conference"**: Proceedings Conference on Religion and Race, 1963, http://www.archive.org/stream/racechallengefor013156m6p/racechallengefor013156mbp-djvv.txt (accessed December 4, 2011).

89 **"We forfeit the right"**: Heschel, *Moral Grandeur and Spiritual Audacity*, vii.

89 **"The day we marched together"**: Susannah Heschel, "Praying with Their Feet: Remembering Abraham Joshua Heschel and Martin Luther King," *Peacework Magazine* 371 (December 2006–January 2007), http://www.peaceworkmaga zine.org/praying-their-feet-remembering-abraham-joshua -heschel-and-martin-luther-king (accessed December 4, 2011).

90 **"I take consolation"**: Heschel, *Moral Grandeur and Spiritual Audacity*, 393.

91 **"Essential in prayer"**: Heschel, *Moral Grandeur and Spiritual Audacity*, 351.

93 **"Hitler . . . did not"**: "Abraham Joshua Heschel," interview by Bob Abernathy, *Religion and Ethics Newsweekly*, January 18, 2008, http://www.pbs.org/wnet/religionandethics/ episodes/january-18-2008/abraham-joshua-heschel/1789.

93 **"For decades"**: Gabrielle Birkner, "Helen Suzman, Barack Obama, and 100 Years of Black-Jewish Relations," *Bintel Blog, Jewish Daily Forward*, January 12, 2009, http://blogs. forward.com/bintel-blog/14913.

94 **"a prophetic figure"**: "Abraham Joshua Heschel," interview by Bob Abernathy, *Religion and Ethics Newsweekly*.

95 **"it's time to do something"**: Lew Feldstein, in discussion with the author, 2000.

99 **"it's important"**: Julius Lester, *Lovesong: Becoming a Jew* (New York: Arcade, 1995), 26.

102 **emergency ethics**: See Michael Walzer, *Arguing about War* (New Haven CT: Yale University Press, 2004).

5. The Fourth Photograph

104 **"ex-Nazi Eichmann goes on trial"**: "Israel: In the Dock," *Time*, April 14, 1961, http://www.time.com/time/magazine/ article/0,9171,872255,00.html.

107 **"worse than Hitler"**: Matthew S. Weinert, "Adolph Eichmann: Understanding Evil in Form and Content," *Human Rights and Human Welfare* 6 (2006): 180.

108 **Despite all efforts"**: Hannah Arendt, *Eichmann in Jerusalem: A Report on the Banality of Evil* (New York: Penguin, 1963), 54.

109 **"Soon after the conquest"**: Rich Cohen, *The Avengers: A Jewish War Story* (New York: Knopf, 2000), 33.

110 **"Clichés, stock phrases"**: Hannah Arendt, *The Life of the Mind* (New York: Harcourt, 1981), 4.

111 **"I admired"**: Adolf Eichmann, "I Transported Them to the Butcher," *Life*, November 28, 1960, 22.

112 **"He agreed to help"**: Adolf Eichmann, "To Sum It All Up, I Regret Nothing," *Life*, December 5, 1960, 146.

113 **"the more important audience"**: "Israel: In the Dock."

115 **read about the killings:** See Alison Mitchell, "West Bank Massacre: At Least 40 Slain in West Bank as Israeli Fires into Mosque," *New York Times*, February 26, 1994, http://www.nytimes.com/1994/02/26/world/west-bank-massacre-least-40-slain-west-bank-israeli-fires-into-mosque-clinton.html?scp=sksq=branchgoldstein.

120 **"anger produces error"**: See "What Anger Causes," adapted by Chaim Miller from the teachings of Lubavitcher Rebbe, *Chabad.org*, http://www.chabad.org/parshah/article_cdo/aid/679194/jewish/What-Anger-Causes.htm.

121 **"This week's *parashah*"**: Rabbi Ismar Schorsch, "Chancellor's Parashah Commentary," July 26, 2003, http://www.jtsa.edu/PreBuilt/ParashahArchives/5763/mattot_masei.shtml.

123 **"Throughout the enlightenment"**: Michael Walzer, "Universalism and Jewish Values," (lecture, Carnegie Council, New York, May 15, 2001), found online at http://www.carnegiecouncil.org/resources/publications/morgenthau/114.html.

135 **"good can be maximized"**: Maurice S. Friedman, *Martin Buber: The Life of Dialogue* (Chicago: University of Chicago Press, 1955), 16.

135 "religious experiences of man": Friedman, *Martin Buber*, 14.

135 "lack of direction": Friedman, *Martin Buber*, 119.

135 "If there were a devil": Friedman, *Martin Buber*, 25.

136 "For two hours": "Israel: Philosopher's Plea," *Time*, March
        23, 1962, http://www.time.com/time/magazine/article/0,91
        71,829108,00.html.

136 "Zion means": Martin Buber, *On Zion: The History of an
        Idea*, trans. Stanley Goodman (New York: Shoken, 1973),
        142.

139 "mission of being Jewish" Interview with the author, July
        2009.

139 population that gives "allegiance": Laura S. Zarembski,
        "Israel's Religious Right—Not a Monolith," *Middle East
        Quarterly* 7, no. 2 (June 2000): 23–31, 24.

140 "Mr. Lieberman spoke": Ira Stoll, "Israel's Lieberman
        Calls for Tougher Stance on Israeli Arabs," *New York Sun*,
        December 13, 2006, http://www.nysun.com/foreign/israels
        -lieberman-calls-for-tougher-stance/45120/.

141 "modern Israeli identity": Avraham Burg, *The Holocaust Is
        Over; We Must Rise from Its Ashes* (New York: Macmillan,
        2008), 100.

141 "It can't work": Shahar Ilan, "Burg Would Have Been Left
        Out," Ha'Aretz, November 6, 2007, http:// www.haaretz
        .com/print-edition/opinion/burg-would-have-been-left-out
        -1.222853.

141 "something other than law": Lotte Kohler and Hans Saner,
        eds., *Hannah Arendt Karl Jaspers*: Correspondence, 1926–
        1969, trans. Robert and Rita Kimber (New York: Harcourt
        Brace, 1992), 418.

142 "Jewish religion": Arendt, *Essays in Understanding, 1930–
        1954*, 18.

6. The Fifth Photograph

144 "after 120 years": Thomas Friedman, "Finds Point to a
        Grander Early Jerusalem," *New York Times*, July 1, 1986,

http://www.nytimes.com/1986/07/01/science/finds-point-to
-a-grander-early-jerusalem.html?pagewanted=all.

146 **"He wanted me to think well"**: Arthur Hertzberg, "A Life-
long Quarrel with God," *New York Times*, May 6, 1990,
http://www.nytimes.com/1990/05/06/books/a-lifelong-quar
rel-with-god.html?pagewanted=all.

147 **"In 622 BCE"**: Jamie S. Korngold, *God in the Wilderness:
Rediscovering the Spirituality of the Great Outdoors with
the Adventure Rabbi* (New York: Three Leaves, 2007), 10.

147 **"monumental discovery"**: Korngold, *God in the Wilderness*,
11.

158 **"Motzkin makes . . . parchment"**: Anthony Weiss, "Female
Torah Scribe Lives off the Land, Religiously," *Jewish Daily
Forward*, January 4, 2008, http://www.forward.com/articles/
12390/.

163 **"Other religions"**: Adin Steinsaltz, *The Thirteen-Petaled
Rose*, trans. Yehuda Hengbi (New York: Basic Books, 1985),
88.

164 **"intellectual study of Torah"**: Steinsaltz, *Thirteen-Petaled
Rose*, 89.

168 **"a story in the Talmud"**: Walter Kaufmann, *From Shake-
speare to Existentialism* (Boston: Beacon, 1959), 179.

178 **"Theology . . . is less central"**: David Hillel Gelernter, *Judaism: A Way of Being* (New Haven CT: Yale University Press,
2009), 5.

179 **"progressive/halachic blend"**: Menachem Creditor, "A Reflection on the Conservative Movement," *The Tisch: Rabbi
Menachem Creditor's Writings*, August 27, 2007, http://rabbi
creditor.blogspot.com/2007/08/reflection-on-conservative-mo
vement.html.

Coda

182 **"This is not"**: Michael Luo, "Jews for Jesus Hit Town and
Find a Tough Crowd," *New York Times*, July 4, 2006, http://

www.nytimes.com/2006/07/04/nyregion/04push.html?page
wanted=print.

182 **"You don't dress up"**: Michelle Boorstein, "Messianic
Group's Touchy Mission," *Washington Post*, June 30, 2007,
http://www.rickross.com/reference/jews_for_jesus/jews_for
_jesus2.html.